Heartbreak to Hope: Overcoming the Anguish of Grief

REV. SAMUEL L. WRIGHT, SR., PH.D.

Copyright © 2016 Rev. Samuel L. Wright, Sr., Ph.D.

All rights reserved.

ISBN: 978-1-941733-91-2

Published by EA Books Publishing a division of
Living Parables of Central Florida, Inc. a 501c3
EABooksPublishing.com

Quotations from the Bible are taken from New Revised Standard Version
Bible, copyright 1989, Division of Christian Education of the National
Council of the Churches of Christ in the United States of America. Used
by permission. All rights reserved.

DEDICATION

To my son Samuel, I miss you, thank God I knew you and hope to embrace you again.

CONTENTS

WHAT HAPPENS WHEN WE DIE?

GRATITUDE & HOPE

ACKNOWLEDGMENTS

I could not have written this book without the support of my wife Yvonne and my daughter Rebekah Joy, who have shared my grief, have read these chapters and have encouraged me to share them with others. I am grateful to my family and especially to my parents, who, having lost a daughter, walked with us after we lost a son. Our church family, Plantation United Methodist Church and clergy friends have been so supportive through this grief process. Special friends Jon & Linda helped us get through the loss of our son Samuel, then lost their son Scott. Thanks are due to the families who lost children, spouses, parents, family and friends, who allowed me, a broken pastor, to have the privilege of walking with them through their grief.

INTRODUCTION

I told a woman at a writers' conference I was working on a book on grief. I explained that I had lost my son and wanted to help people deal with their grief by sharing my journey. I related to her that as a pastor, I had walked with many people through their time of sorrow, and I hoped this book would help many more.

She immediately pulled me aside, away from her husband, and said, "Nothing is going to be said about this after I tell you what I am about to say."

Seemed to be a strange way to begin a conversation with someone she had just met. "I lost two children," she said. "At the time I felt like nobody in the world knew how I felt. I thought I would go crazy. I prayed and prayed, but could not get any relief."

This book is for her. And for all of us like her. Not that it can take anyone's pain away, but so we can know that others walk the path of anguish. She is not alone. I am not alone. Although grief makes us feel isolated, you are not alone.

This book is for parents who have lost children, wives who have lost husbands, and husbands — wives, siblings who have lost a brother or sister, grandparents who have lost grandchildren. The list could go on and on, from the death of best friends to grandparents, from co-workers to fiancés.

As a seasoned pastor, I've traveled alongside many who have struggled with terrible loss. In the two years since our son's death,

I've sought to comfort the mother whose daughter was murdered, the young couple whose daughter died in the womb, and the family of the young woman who died in her bed at home after a routine surgery. I've spent time talking with the sons and wife of the man who died from a stroke while working out at the gym, with the couple whose 18-year-old daughter did not wake up one morning, with our friends whose son lost his battle with cancer, and with the family of the man who lost his fight with liver disease before his fortieth birthday. I've offered my presence to the family of the little girl who died unexpectedly just before her first birthday, and to the widow whose husband had been afflicted with Alzheimer's for years.

I write out of my own grief, their anguish and the sorrow of many others I have known. I write for them and for our family in the loss of Matt and Tina, who died far too young, and Len, who died by suicide. I write for all who grieve.

Why Read This Book?

First, you will know you are not alone in grief. While it is true that no two people are alike and no two losses are the same, it may help to know that I struggle as you do. The distraught woman at the conference felt no one else knew the pain she experienced in losing two children. She did not even want her husband to hear her conversation with me. Was he tired of hearing about it? Was it too painful for him to discuss? Had she ever shared with him how she felt? I'm not sure. But I know she felt alone in her grief. As we all do at some point.

Second, even though each grief is unique, all humans suffer grief in similar ways. So we can learn how to be there for each other. Two months after our son's death, I went to a previously scheduled clergy retreat. One of the pastors, who had lost his son years before, came over to me before our meeting began. He gave me a big hug. That simple loving gesture brought a depth of connection and comfort that greatly encouraged me. I knew that he had gone through deep sorrow, that he shared my pain, and that he understood. He reached out to me. As you read this book, I pray that you will feel God's loving arms around you.

2

Third, this book will show you that it's okay to doubt that God exists. It's okay to be angry with God. I am an active pastor, a former missionary and seminary professor. Yet I experienced "the dark night of the soul" in which God seems to be absent. By my opening my heart and life, I'll show you it's normal to have doubts and issues with God.

Fourth, I invite you to join me on this most difficult trek as a friend. We are in this together. Although I cannot be with you in person, I hope we can connect through these words. I am a pastor; however, I cannot take the place of your pastor. If you do not have a pastor, priest, psychologist, counselor, or a good friend, I highly recommend finding one. I offer this book as a small way of making the journey with you, sharing my pain, relating to what you are going through, and making suggestions that may help.

By sharing a little of my struggle, connecting with Scripture, offering words of comfort and encouragement, including suggestions and a prayer, my hope is that God's grace will become evident in your life in spite of your agony.

Learning How to Grieve

Before you read any further, I invite you to do a simple exercise. Grasp some object in your hands, anything, the back of a chair, the edge of a table, a book. Clench your hands tight on it for ten seconds, as hard as you can. Now release your grip and let your hands relax by your side for ten seconds. That simple act of holding on and letting go is an object lesson of how we get through grief.

At the most basic and painful level, grief is about letting go of someone we love. It sounds simple, but nothing is more difficult. To get through the worst parts of mourning, we also have to learn to let go of denial, anger, sadness, guilt, and more. That said, getting through sorrow also involves holding on, holding on: to the people we love, to memories of those we have lost, and to God. We hang on to hope, to love, and to faith.

If we do not learn how to grieve, how to let go, and to hold on, we may end up hurting others or ourselves. Not learning how to grieve has broken up marriages, caused people to die by suicide, caused the permanent estrangement of siblings, led to vengeful murders, and even prompted attacks between nations. It's important to be able to get through this difficult ordeal, to survive in a way that allows for the least amount of harm, in a way that moves us toward hope and healing.

We have no training in how to grieve. No one prepared us for this difficult journey. When loss slams us down, we are in shock. We immediately begin a crash course in how to wrestle with grief. It is a complex and tortuous journey. I wish I could offer a book with six simple steps for overcoming grief. If only it were that easy. The most powerful way I can help you is to share my struggle. By showing you my journey from heartbreak to hope, it is my prayer that you may have more light on your path through the "dark night of the soul."

I cannot fix your pain. This book cannot take away your loss. My prayer is that reading it may help.

In going through the anguish of the loss of my son, it became obvious to me that many people are ignorant about grief. As a pastor for many years I had walked with people enduring terrible sorrow. Yet I found I had much to learn about the experience of loss. I still do. People said things to us during our time of misery that revealed a complete lack of understanding of what grief is and how people mourn. Well-meaning people and even highly educated people seem to have no clue about grief. I have seen a great deal of damage done to others by what people have said, or left unsaid.

Christian people would use biblical passages to try to cheer us up or straighten us out. The theology behind their thinking seemed shallow and unrealistic to me. For example, they might quote the Apostle Paul, "Rejoice in the Lord always, and again I say rejoice" (Phil. 4:4). Or the "joy of the Lord is my strength" (Neh. 8:10). They would say that a Christian should always have the joy of the Lord. Really? To me it sounded like they were saying you should always be happy even in loss. That did not seem realistic to me.

As humans we suffer deeply when we experience loss. Was Jesus joyful when his cousin John was executed or when Jesus sweated drops of blood in the Garden before his arrest, torture, and crucifixion? Was he happy when he cried out from the cross, "My God, my God why have you forsaken me?" (Mark 15:34) This

4

pretending always to be positive and joyful seems to be a form of Christian denial, not at all real, a kind of pseudo spirituality.

Scripture

In my ministry, both as a pastor and as a seminary professor in Biblical Studies, I have found that people overlook parts of the Bible that do not bolster their biases. Stories about loss, songs of lament, and prayers for relief from the burden of grief, fill the pages of the Bible. Often these resources have been ignored when it comes to how Christians think about loss. Instead of quoting verses to tell people to stop grieving and be happy, perhaps we should listen to the larger biblical witness with regard to people going through the pain of loss.

In the story of Adam and Eve, these first parents lost their first two sons when the older Cain killed the younger Abel, then ran away. Mary, the mother of Jesus, watched her son die on a cross. From the enslavement of Israelites to the persecution of the early church, whole groups of people suffered in the Bible. As a student and teacher of the Bible, I think it is important to acknowledge this pain in the pages of Scripture, something we often ignore. However, the final word in the Bible is not loss, grief or death. In the end the news is good: God comforts us in the midst of despair, assures us in a flood of doubt and promises resurrection in the face of death. God is our hope.

It is those of us who have gone through the deepest valleys, who have come to know the deepest comfort of God. No one would choose to endure such pain. However, the healing grace of God would not be known without such heartache. There is no joy of the resurrection without the heartache of the crucifixion. I tend to ignore Good Friday in favor of Easter. Every Sunday is a mini-Easter. Good Friday is remembered only once a year. I like it that way. Let's emphasize the positive.

When death takes someone we love, we are living Good Friday every day. We are chained to the foot of the cross. We wail and weep with Mary as she watches her son in agony and death. The story does not end there. As Christians, our hope is in the resurrection, the hope of eternal life. However, living into that hope challenges all of us in the anguish of loss.

What Happened?

My cell phone vibrated on the table as I was digging into the fried chicken breast at the men's meeting in the fellowship hall. I picked it up and answered. My daughter Rebekah Joy blurted out, "Samuel has been killed. You need to come home." I jumped up to leave.

The president of the men's group was sitting next to me. He asked if everything was okay. I mumbled, "No," as I rushed to the door.

I drove home to the parsonage in disbelief. After the three of us embraced for a long time with lots of sobbing, my wife Yvonne said that she had gotten a call from the Los Angeles Coroner's Office. The officer said that our 32-year-old son, Samuel, had been killed in a crash while riding his motorcycle on the Angeles Forest Highway. News of his death began the worst time of my life.

As a motorcycle courier in Los Angeles, our son Samuel rode a motorcycle for a living. He had ridden more than 200,000 miles in five-and-a-half years at his job. He loved flying on the white line between the cars, zipping through the traffic to deliver legal documents to beat a deadline. This is perfectly legal in California.

The white line is a legal lane for motorcycles. He was on his way to work, from Lancaster to Los Angeles, an hour-and-a-half commute on his favorite canyon road, Angeles Forest Highway. He and thousands of motorcyclists ride this road for fun each weekend during the summer. On Monday morning May 20, 2013, he crashed into a mountain. He was killed instantly. We don't know why he crashed. We still have lots of questions.

Permission to Grieve

I write this book as one who has suffered loss in part for you to give yourself permission to grieve—something our society is reluctant to do. In my own struggle I have encountered Christians who insist we "put on a happy face" no matter the depths of loss. For them to be down or depressed is be unspiritual, to fail. God wants us to be positive, to always smile—even if it's fake?

No. God wants us to be honest, to be real. It is only in the confession of our pain and loss, our weakness and heartache, that we discover a Savior. It is only when we shake our fists in anger at God that we begin to see the depths of God's gentleness and grace. It is in our humanity that we find the deepest spirituality because God made us in our Creator's own image.

How to Read This Book

I would never read more than a chapter of this book at a time. But that's me. Read it any way what works for you. Each chapter stands alone. They do not have to be read in order. Try the suggested actions or reflections. They may actually help. I write as a friend who has suffered, willing to walk with you in your anguish. Let's walk together down this rocky path.

This book would be ideal for discussion in a grief support group. I have included discussion questions at the end of the book to facilitate groups using this book. Of course, these questions could also be helpful for individuals.

HEARTBREAK

1 Abused by Grief

Be gracious to me, O LORD, for I am in distress;
my eye wastes away from grief,
my soul and body also.
For my life is spent with sorrow,
and my years with sighing;
my strength fails because of my misery,
and my bones waste away.
Psalm 31:9-10

As this ancient psalm shows, sadness, sorrow and fatigue are not new to the human family. We can relate to the psalmist's grief and despair because we have been beaten up by grief.

Like a roller coaster, our emotions jerk us in one direction, then the other. Our grief drives us straight down, then drags us back up. The emotions in many psalms go up and down, back and forth, even in the same paragraph. The Psalms are not linear, just as our emotions in grief are not. When one suffers, language and thought patterns are not enough to communicate the depth of despair and grief. We don't color within the lines of standard communications. Our experience out runs our human language.

Abused by Grief

It has been ten months since
Our son Samuel was killed.

In the beginning the
Monstrous gorilla
Pounced on me
Beating my chest
With one massive fist,
Smothering
My face with his other
Without a moment's relief.

The towering brute
Shook me like a rag doll
Dragged me by the hair
From one side of the cage
To the other;
Tossed me around
Stomped me down
Picked me up by the throat
Squeezed the life out of me.

This teething giant
Chomped on me like a human chew toy.
My face pressed against
The bars as he pounded my back.
No escape from his fury
No strength to endure
No hope.

I could not breathe.
I could not rest.
I could not fight back.
I could not sleep.
I could not heal.
Locked in the cage
With this massive foe.

9

We sit in the cage together
Now that I'm able to sit up
Still with considerable pain.
My wounds have scabbed over.
He raises his fist and I flinch
In the corner.
His yellow eyes smile.
His glare terrifies me
Into total submission
Which satisfies Grief
Most of the time.

But like Samson
My hair is growing back
I have regained some strength.
I managed to stand,
Which resulted in a severe beating.
Grief suffers no competition.

Lying on my back
Through bloodied eyes
I notice
This cage has no roof!
Escape might be possible.
But the bars are too high
I am too weak
To shinny up them.

I measure the enormous
Primate whose back is toward me.
He is leaning forward looking out the bars
Staring into the darkness.
His massive furry skull
Nearly reaches the top.

Could I use Grief
Like a ramp
To climb out of

This torture chamber?
I have to be quick.
No room for a running start.
I have to try.

I am learning there is no way to avoid the gorilla in the cage. I have to go through the grief. There are no shortcuts. I tried to postpone grieving. I only took two days off before returning to work in the administrative aspects of being a senior pastor in a large church. Two weeks after our son's death, I worked an 80-hour week—not that unusual for me.

Over the years I had walked with many people through their grief, but I did not know how to grieve. So I avoided it. People around me, including our Staff-Parish Relations Committee and my wife, encouraged me to take time off to grieve, but I chose not to. I am still learning how to grieve today.

Encouragement

Each of us must find our path through the valley. I had to find mine. You have to find yours. There is no right or wrong here. Pain is inescapable.

Sometimes people avoid grieving for years. Something happens, another loss or traumatic event. Then they find themselves face to face with the gorilla. Their logic tells them this has already been dealt with, yet the pain of their broken hearts erupts like lava running down the slopes of the volcano. Denying grief does not make it dormant. Unless you let it out, deal with the pain and work through your grief, it is still there to grapple. Below I offer some suggestions. Pick and choose what might be helpful for you—or ignore them all and do your own thing. But find a way to work through your grief.

Moving Forward

1. See a counselor in an ongoing discussion of your grief.

2. Join a support group for those who are grieving. Check out Compassionate Friends (loss of a child, www.compassionatefriends.org) , GriefShare (loss of any loved one, www.griefshare.org) or local support groups for widows and widowers.

11

3. Read and reflect on Psalm 31.

4. Treat yourself to a massage to help relieve the stress of grief.

Prayer
Lord, help us to traverse the valley of the shadow of death. Give us courage to journey through grief. Cradle us in your arms as we endure the pain of loss. Instill in us hope that one day we will be through the hardest part, that things will get easier. May we experience your grace even in the midst of heartache. Amen.

2 Letting Go

*O Most High,
when I am afraid,
I put my trust in you.
In God, whose word I praise,
in God I trust; I am not afraid;
what can flesh do to me?*
Psalm 56:2b-4a

The psalmist encourages himself with positive affirmations about not being afraid, when he clearly is afraid. His pronouncements of faith are intended to encourage himself and the community of faith. How hard it is to trust God especially when we go through grief! Our confidence in God and in ourselves is often shaken. We need to encourage ourselves and one another to let go of fear.

Let Go of the Bar!

I lost my son months ago.
He's gone.
But I can't let go.

Letting go feels like
Betrayal
Of his memory
Of his life.

Letting go feels like
Throwing my little boy
Into the river
Teeming with alligators

Like leaving him alone
Bleeding by the side
Of Angeles Forest
Highway

Like abandoning my
Baby to the snow and cold,
Like losing him
All over again.

But is it for him that
I hold on?
He is gone.
It does him no good.

What disservice do I
Accomplish if I let go?
Am I less of a father
If I release him?

What do I hold on to?
The memory?
The loss?
The pain?

How do I do this letting go?
Do I try to forget the pain?
Do I ignore my brokenness?
Do I stop grieving?

I am frozen in time
Suspended by my knees
On the bar of the trapeze
At the height of my swing

14

My arms outstretched
My hands ready
To catch my son as he flies
Toward me.

I am the catcher.
That's what fathers do.
I have always caught him.
I have never missed.

Though my catches
Were not perfect,
I never missed him.
I never let go.
Never let him fall.

But now his bar
Dangles far below me
Barely moving.
Empty.

I'm still waiting
Frozen at the end of my arc
Calling out to him
"Don't be afraid.
You have to let go.
I will catch you."

My words echo
Off the empty
Circus tent
Back to me.

"Don't be afraid."

"You have to let go."

"I will catch you."

But I've never been
The one who is caught,
Never practiced
Flying through the air
Letting go of the bar.

How can the catcher
Become the one
Who is caught?

Suddenly I'm swinging
Hard, fast
Backward through the air
My speed builds

Then as I sail up high
Near the roof of the canvas
I hear a voice call out.

"Don't be afraid.
You have to let go.
You be the son.
I'll be the Father."

I am learning to let go—to let go of tears and let them flow. I am learning to let go of control because I have no control over what happens. I am learning to let go of fear of what might happen in light of our loss. It's hard to let go and to trust God. Yet it is part of my grief process. My experience of loss has been like falling through fog, not knowing when I'll crash to the ground or if there will be a net to catch me. Accepting that reality for me means letting go of fear, sadness, and anger.

Encouragement
Grief is a process of letting go of the way things used to be and learning to embrace the new normal. It takes time to let go of the fear, the anger, the sadness, and the heartache. Yet it is only when we let go of pain that we can reach for comfort. It is only as we release our hands off the bar of heartache that we can begin to

take hold of the extended arms of God's peace. This letting go is something that you can learn to do even if you've never done it before. It seems to take forever, but you can do it. You can get through this.

Moving Forward
1. Take several small pieces of paper. Write slowly on one "Pain." Crumple the paper. Then drop it into a recycling bin. Then pray, "God help me let go of my pain." Repeat this for "Anger," "Sadness," "Confusion," "Bitterness," or whatever you need to release. If it would be more helpful, drop each piece of crumpled paper into a burning fire.

2. Get more active with the first idea. If you have old golf balls, write the words on several of them and hit them into a lake. I don't shoot skeet, but I think one helpful thing to do would be to shout, "Pull" and then say "Pain" or "Sadness" as you squeeze the trigger to obliterate each clay as a symbol of letting go.

3. Read and reflect on Psalm 56.

Prayer
God of love, help us to let go of our anguish. Inspire us to release the heartache as we fall into your loving embrace. Amen.

3 No Call Today

The king was deeply moved, and went up to the chamber over the gate, and wept; and as he went, he said, "O my son Absalom, my son, my son Absalom! Would I had died instead of you, O Absalom, my son, my son!"
2 Samuel 18:33

David mourned his son Absalom's death. This is the normal reaction of a father who has lost a son. King David wept.

What is unusual about the situation is that Absalom had actually led an insurrection against his father David. He had taken over David's throne and was in pursuit of David and his army.

David's men managed to kill Absalom. No doubt, Absalom would have killed David had he gotten the chance. Incredibly, in spite of his son's rebellion, at his son's death, David mourned like a typical father.

No Call Today

Today is Father's Day.
No phone call.
No celebrating
My being his father
He was killed in a crash.
Taken in an instant
He's been gone four weeks
Nothing to celebrate.

18

Today is his birthday.
I cannot call him from the condo
On the beach where we celebrated
His birthday every year when
He was growing up.
We are there.
He is not.

No call
No card
No gift
No son
No celebration of his
Birth 33 years ago.
Only grief at his
Death, a new grief, just
Two months old.

His sister's birthday today.
He would have called.
Six months ago
They had talked
At length.
For her it's the big Three Zero.

With his death
She will never receive
Her most desired gift
A closer bond with
Her brother,
Her only sibling.
No long chat today.

Today is my birthday.
But I will not get that
Annual celebratory call.
No teasing about my
Getting old.

Instead we nurture a
Six-month-old
Grief.

Thanksgiving has come
And gone
No call
An empty seat
At the bountiful feast.

He had plans for Christmas
He was taking his girlfriend
Camping out in the
California desert,
A place he loved.

No cell coverage there
He would have called
Before they left.
Instead he has
Deserted
Her
Us.

O dreaded month of May,
Today is Mother's Day
The last time she talked
With him
A year ago.
No call today.

Today is her birthday.
No call today.
No teasing.
No best wishes.
No love expressed,
Only love remembered
And lost.

Today is the anniversary
Of the phone call
His mother received
From the Los Angeles
County Coroner,
A nightmare phone call
Every parent dreads,
Telling us our son
Is dead.

He will not call today.
He will call never again.
Gaping hole
Empty ache.

All these days of celebration
Have become instead
Deserts of loneliness
With howling winds
By night
Dead silence
By day

In the heavy silence
Our ears remain alert
To his call that
Never comes.

I am learning that even for a guy it's okay to weep, to cry. Jesus wept.

Many of us think weeping is a sign of weakness. Rather, crying means we're human. Often we equate strength with stoically holding all our emotions in, being in control so that no one sees us crack.

In the history of the world there has never been a warrior equal to David. King Saul, who was a head taller than all his men, was a mighty fighter in battle. As the old song went, "Saul has killed his thousand, but David his tens of thousands." (1 Sam. 18:7) In the ancient world Israelites and later Jews had a reputation for being the best warriors, the fiercest fighters. David was the strongest of the strong, the bravest of the brave.

Yet David wept over the death of his son, something parents do when they lose a child—even if that child has disappointed them; even if that child has opposed them or done evil to them. I am learning to weep.

Encouragement

Give yourself permission to express your emotions in any way that seems natural for you. Cry! Weep! Sob! Wail! Cry in front of people, by yourself—whenever your emotions overwhelm you. It's okay. Don't be ashamed of your tears. Ignore those who look down on you for being human. Remember their lack of emotion is not strength.

Jesus said we are to weep with those who weep. Jesus gave us permission to cry, to cry with others and seek out those who will cry with us. If someone cannot weep with you, is it a sign of strength or a lack of empathy? If tears do not come to their eyes too, is it that their is faith greater than yours or that they cannot express love for you? Cut them some slack. They do not understand. But cut yourself even more slack in your grief. Be yourself, as God created you with all your emotions. Let them call you a "basket case."

David was a "basket case" when his troops killed his enemy, his son Absalom. David's general, Joab, criticized David for his display of emotions in his grief, for turning a day of victory into a day of mourning. Grief does that. Not only was David a great warrior, he was "a man after God's own heart." (1 Sam. 13:14) Apparently men and women after God's own heart weep in their grief. Cry and ignore the critics.

Our tears are precious to God. God collects our tears according to the psalmist: "You have kept count of my tossings; put my tears in your bottle. Are they not in your record?" (Psalm 56:8)

Moving Forward

1. Set aside some time for grief in a place where you can cry undisturbed.

2. Find a counselor or friend with whom you can talk and who will be present with you if you break down in your grief.

3. Read and reflect on Psalm 3.

Prayer
God, who created us in your image with all your emotions from joyful ecstasy to utter despair, help us to be free to cry in our own grief and to weep with those who weep in their grief. Help us to let the tears flow as we mourn our loss, knowing our tears are precious to you. Amen.

4 Will I Ever Feel Better?

How long, O LORD? Will you forget me forever?
How long will you hide your face from me?
How long must I bear pain in my soul,
and have sorrow in my heart all day long?
Psalm 13:1-2a

Deep grief lasts so long. It feels even longer. It was weeks and weeks before I was not thinking of my son's death when I went to bed and when I woke up. The loss was overwhelming. The days were long, the nights longer. After a few months I began to ask myself, "Will I ever feel better? Will I ever be happy again?" The heartache drags on and on.

Crushing Waves

The raging storm
Of grief
Drives the waves
Knocking me down
Grinding me on the sands
Of the beach.

They come so
Often I am down
More than
I walk.

24

No progress.

Sometimes I just
Lie there
As the waves crash
Over me
Allowing the
Salt water
To multiply my tears
And the beach
To sand my skin raw.

Is there no end
To this stretch of sand
That conspires with the
Tidal beast
To lay me down?

Is his desire
To drag me out
Into the abyss
To claim another victim?

Once a vibrant
Tree full of leaves
And fruit
I am tossed like a
Bleached branch
Of driftwood with
Seaweed for leaves
Barnacles for fruit,
A caricature of
What once was.

Why?
Why trudge along this strip
Of sand
Imprisoned
Between grief

And loneliness?

The sun is out now.
Months have passed.
I'm still constrained
To walk along
Grief's edge.

The beach rash
Is healing
But rogue waves
Still overwhelm me
Landing on me
Without warning
Like a sick whale beaching
On top of me.

Now I have the strength
To squeeze out from under
To get back up
And lumber on.
Most days.

I claw my way
Back each time.
Shedding threads of
Seaweed
Sadness
Trudging on.

Now and again
At night
The wind dies down.
The waves become
Ripples.

The moon glistens
Silver as I stop,
Sit and wonder

If this gentle light has
Always been there,
If peace and calm
May linger,
If there is still
Hope.

I'm learning it does get better. We may feel like the psalmist, that the pain is going on forever. But there is hope that with the help of God and compassion of others, the sadness will eventually not overwhelm. Yes, there will always be sadness about our loss, but when we move on to accept what has happened, peace will eventually visit us.

Healing and peace will come, even if very slowly. Time does not heal all wounds. But with time healing can come if we allow ourselves to be comforted, if we make ourselves trudge through all this pain and heartache and not get swallowed up by it. There are no shortcuts. The painful road is long. However, little by little the raw pain of grief subsides.

Encouragement

You will feel better. Life will never be the same after a significant loss, but you will eventually feel less acute pain. The waves of grief will knock you down less often. You will be able to function better with time.

Moving Forward

1. Read the following passage aloud. (Jesus quoted this passage as he characterized his ministry in his sermon in his hometown of Nazareth.)

> *The spirit of the Lord GOD is upon me,*
> *because the LORD has anointed me;*
> *he has sent me to bring good news to the oppressed,*
> *to bind up the brokenhearted,*
> *to proclaim liberty to the captives,*
> *and release to the prisoners;*
> *to proclaim the year of the LORD'S favor,*
> *and the day of vengeance of our God;*
> *to comfort all who mourn;*

27

to provide for those who mourn in Zion —
to give them a garland instead of ashes,
the oil of gladness instead of mourning,
the mantle of praise instead of a faint spirit. (Isaiah 61:1-3a)

2. Reflect on how the Spirit of the Lord is still among us to comfort those of us who mourn. Can you see any evidence in your life of God slowly helping you overcome the worst parts of your grief? Have you ever considered that God's mission is to bind up your broken heart?

Prayer
God of comfort and peace, embrace all of us who struggle with grief. Carry us through this difficult time. Like a shepherd, lead us to the still waters and cure our mangled souls. Amen.

5 Cruel Calendar

In the ninth year of King Zedekiah of Judah, in the tenth month, King Nebuchadrezzar of Babylon and all his army came against Jerusalem and besieged it; in the eleventh year of Zedekiah, in the fourth month, on the ninth day of the month, a breach was made in the city. When Jerusalem was taken, all the officials of the king of Babylon came and sat in the middle gate . . . .
Jeremiah 39:1-3a

The ninth of the Jewish month of Av is a fast day in Judaism (Tisha B'Av). It commemorates the fall of Jerusalem and the destruction of the first temple in 587 BCE mentioned above in Jeremiah 39. The destruction of the second temple in 70 CE and other calamities that Jewish people have experienced are also remembered on this day every year.

As groups of people we have days that we remember with pain. September 11th, has become such a day for citizens of the United States because of the attacks of that day in 2001 and the thousands of lives lost. In our families we also have days that remind us of our sorrow.

Grief drags us down as we mark a week, a month, a year, and so on, since our loss. Dates that had no previous meaning suddenly become the most prominent on the calendar — and not in a good way.

Cruel Calendar

Does every month
Have to have a 20th?

A wave of grief
Will lie in wait,
Even when I forget
The date,
Slam me down
Drag me through
The time of terror
When my world turned
Dark, black as night
No stars, no moon
No street light
No hand in front of my face.

Why can't I change
My calendar
To erase the 20th of
Every month,
Delete every
Monday evening
When the coroner called?

Let me blot out
May entirely.
This year:
May 6, Baby Leah
May 10, Ed dies
May 11, Jay dies
May 17, Brad dies
May 26, Matt dies

Add the darkened dates of previous Mays.
May 19, Johnny killed at 25
May 20, Samuel's crash
May 26, Len's suicide

30

May 26, G-Mamma dies

Perhaps my wife
Would also vote to
Drop the month
Of her birth
Of Mother's day.
The weight of grief
Eclipses little joys.
The dark wind
Snuffs out the candles
On our soggy cakes.

But then
What of June?
The month for brides and burials
Memorials and funerals
Scott, Samuel, Matt, Len . . .
Shall we toss out the
Wedding anniversaries
With the days
We were outside the church
Breathing out sobs,
Not blowing bubbles?

Then there is July
More days marked by death
Tina's birthday
Samuel's birthday
Scott's birthday
All gone
Reminders of joys
Forever past.

Every month
Bares the scars
Of death and loss.

Rather than mark

31

The passing of time
The Xed-out numbers
On the calendar
Chisel in our souls
The loss of life
Of loves.

Why can't we have
These dark days
Off the record
So that their numbers
Do not keep coming
Back around
Like a carousel
Of monsters
Jabbing at us
Laughing at our pain?

Like the "hump-day" camel
In the stupid commercial
Asking "Do you know what day it is?"
The Grim Reaper
Grabs more and more
Days and dates
To flash his scythe
In our faces on these
Numbered squares
Burned into our brains
Tattooed on our souls.

He asks,
"Do you know what
Day it is?
It's the day I took him.
It's the day you lost her.
Your day will come."

To which we respond,
"It already has."

32

Although it sounds simplistic, these dates come and must be endured. They have been hard, often harder than I expected. Emotions have surprised me. I've observed that sometimes I was not even aware of the date consciously until my emotions reminded my rational side of the date. "Why am I so sad today? O, yes, of course. It's the 20th."

I also realized that many others will not understand. They will think we are silly for having a bad day just because time marks a month, two months, or a year. They may not say it, but they communicate, "Get over it. After all it's been a whole month, or two or three, or a year, or two or three." I even have chided myself for not getting past this grief on some silly time frame, which I, or others, have imposed. "It takes as long as it takes." The first time I heard that I thought it sounded stupid. But now I know.

There is no standard of "thirty days and you will feel better." It's not like getting over bronchitis. There is no antibiotic to speed up the process. A broken heart takes a long time to get better and even then some fissures never completely heal.

Encouragement

You may not think so, but you can endure this. It is survivable. Ignore your own invented timetable for getting better. Give yourself grace to grieve—whatever time you need. It does get easier. However, because it takes so long, sometimes you feel like it will never get better. And there are days even long afterward, when the sadness is just as strong as in the beginning. But those sad days are not as long as at first; nor do they come as often.

Moving Forward

It may be helpful to begin traditions to commemorate the anniversaries of your loved one's death. When you are able, find a way to mark the days in ways that remember and honor the one you lost. Allow yourself time and space to grieve and to heal.

1. Light a candle each month on that day in their memory.

2. Go out to eat their favorite kind of food. Cook their favorite meal.

3. On the anniversary, schedule the day off to spend with those who were closest to you and to them. Look through photos.

4. Do an activity you enjoyed doing together.

5. On their birthday bake the cake/cookie/dessert they loved.

6. Read and reflect on Psalm 90.

Prayer
God, mend our broken hearts. As the calendar reminds us of our loss, help us to be patient as we endure this long suffering on our way to being healed. Give us the confidence that it will get better in your mercy. Amen.

6 The Deeper the Love

*How the mighty have fallen
in the midst of the battle!
Jonathan lies slain upon your high places.
I am distressed for you, my brother Jonathan;
greatly beloved were you to me;
your love to me was wonderful,
passing the love of women.
How the mighty have fallen,
and the weapons of war perished!*
2 Samuel 1:25-27

When David got news that King Saul and his son Jonathan had been killed in battle, David mourned. David included both Saul and Jonathan in his lament, but one gets the feeling that the mourning for King Saul's death was partly for political reasons. After all, Saul had been his enemy and David wanted to rule Saul's kingdom. But the mourning for Jonathan feels like it comes from the depth of David's soul. They loved each other deeply.

Deep grief grows out of deep love. Whether it is a spouse, a child, a sibling, a friend, or relative, the anguish is multiplied by the love in the hearts of those who survive.

Love One Another!

"Love one another!"
Such is the command of Christ.

What you did not say, Lord,
Was that to obey would mean
My heart would be
Ripped from my chest.

The amputation of my soul
Comes one limb at a time
For each one I have loved
And lost.

It would have been better
Not to have loved
Not to have cherished
Not to have given my
Heart away!

For now my heart has
Been crushed
By the loss of love.

As David mourned
The loss of his loyal
Friend, Jonathan,
I mourn the loss of
My loyal son, Samuel.

Part of me is missing--
Not like the piece from
The puzzle nearly completed, but
More like the loss of a hand
Whose absence is a
Constant incapacity.

The arm of my soul
Reaches out
To take,
To touch,
To help,
But there are no fingers

36

No palm, no thumb
To fulfill
The heart's purpose.

The scarred stump
Serves only to testify
Of what once was.

There should have been
A disclaimer with
This command to love.
Could you not warn us
That the greater the love
The greater the heartache?

Why do these oak roots
Of love dive so deep
Into our being?
When our loved one dies,
The massive hole
Reveals all the little
Entanglements of love,
All the broken connections
Now exposed.
We wither in
The scorching sun.

The gaping hole
That is left
Swallows
Everything.

Love one another?
Where is the disclaimer
Telling us what love
May cost us?

The CROSS!

I am learning that my grief is directly related to how much I love. The devastation of losing my son matches the love I had for him. The only way for me not to grieve so deeply would be for me not to have loved him so much.

Perhaps it is not consoling, although it is enlightening, to know we feel the pain deeply because we love deeply. The crater left in our souls due to our loss would not be there if our hearts had not been filled to the brim with love.

God is love. God encourages us to love, so we take this risk with each person to whom we give our hearts, that we may be devastated at their death. The alternative—not loving anyone so that we may not be hurt if we lose her, him—would lead to a lonely existence.

Encouragement
When we suffer deep loss, there is a part of us that wants to withdraw completely, like a turtle into its shell. That way we will not be hurt again. If that helps to be a hermit to heal, that's okay. However, don't we have to risk it all again by loving someone else eventually?

Moving Forward
1. Read and reflect on the "Song of the Bow "in 2 Samuel 1:17-27.

2. Reflect on these questions:
   - Did I ever imagine it would hurt so much to lose someone I loved?
   - Is loving worth the risk to me?
   - Should I guard my heart more in the future?
   - How would my death impact others?
   - How can I take Jesus as my model?

Prayer
Dear God, you are love. You love each of us more than we can fathom. We are taught to mourn with those who mourn. Does that mean that your grief surpasses all of ours? We imagine you walking with us, crying with us, sharing our pain because of your great love for us. Thank you for loving us and grieving with us. Amen.

7 Moving On Without Me

My God, my God, why have you forsaken me?
Why are you so far from helping me, from the words of my groaning?
O my God, I cry by day, but you do not answer;
and by night, but find no rest.
Psalm 22:1-2

Jesus quotes the first line of this psalm as he is dying on the cross. No doubt he felt abandoned by God as he died a cruel death. All of us feel abandoned in many different ways when we suffer the death of a loved one.

Abandoned

I scream but no one hears
I'm pulled below the surface
By the undertow of grief.

Kicking upward
I catch a glimpse of them leaving the beach
As I am drowning in my sadness.
They were there for me
For a while
But now they are
Moving on.

I lunge toward them

39

But it's awkward.
They are over it
Past it.

My friends stayed with me
Walked with me in my grief for a time.
What a comfort they have been!

But the burden of grief is
Too great to bear
For those who do not own it.
And owning it
Means letting others move on.

I sink downward
Shackled to steel chains of sadness
Enveloped by gathered tears
Of salty heartaches.

Back to your cars!
Back to your lives!
Back away from the edge of the abyss
Lest you fall into this
Watery grave with me!

The sun is still shining bright
For you
But the light is disappearing
As I drop deeper and deeper.

Why would I want you to drown
With me?
You are my friends.
Do not join me
In Poseidon's prison!

Seaweed
Slithers through my hair.
Darkness closes around my heart.

Jagged coral cuts my skin.
Shadows circle overhead.
The weight of my coffin presses
Against my chest
Grinding my back against
The grainy lining.

But death,
Who has robbed me
Of the core of my heart,
Does not take me.

Like ancient Jonah
I am vomited out
On the beach of my despair
Now dark and deserted.

Still grasped by iron grief
Whose grip has not weakened
Though aged
With rust
Covered
With barnacles
All turned blue.

My son and I played a trick on my wife and daughter once or twice. While we were traveling on long trips we stopped at a gas station for a pit stop. They took longer in the bathroom than we did. When we came out to the car, we got this brilliant idea. We moved the car to the other side of the parking lot where we could see them come out of the restrooms, but not so visible to them. Then when they came out, we watched as they looked for the car.

It was hilarious--for us. We only let their confusion and disorientation last for a minute then I would drive over to them. My wife did not think it was funny. In fact, we only did it once (well maybe twice) because her reaction was so strong. We all fear abandonment. Grief overwhelms us with that feeling.

Encouragement

As you grieve, you may feel you have been abandoned by your loved one. Many people feel angry with the one who has died for this very reason. You may feel abandoned by God. God was not there for you or for your loved one, or at least that is how it feels. You may feel left behind by others who have moved on with their lives and think you should be over it by now.

Feelings are neither right nor wrong, they just are. Feeling abandoned terrorizes us during grief. This feeling of abandonment may be stronger than you have ever felt before. You can learn to live with this discomfort, to acknowledge you feel abandoned and begin to let it go.

Moving Forward

1. If you are feeling abandoned, write a letter to God honestly describing your feelings and asking for a sense of his presence.

2. Write a letter to the one who has passed away telling them why you miss them. As difficult as this may be, it can help you deal with buried emotions.

3. Set up a meeting with a counselor, friend, psychologist, or pastor to discuss these feelings of being abandoned.

4. Read and reflect on Psalm 38.

Prayer

Lord, you promised to always be with us. Yet, we feel like you have abandoned us. It hurts to think you have let go of us and let us down. Comfort us with your loving presence as we grieve. Amen.

42

8 The Hardest Thing

Therefore, since we are surrounded by so great a cloud of witnesses, let us also lay aside every weight and the sin that clings so closely, and let us run with perseverance the race that is set before us, looking to Jesus the pioneer and perfecter of our faith, who for the sake of the joy that was set before him endured the cross, disregarding its shame, and has taken his seat at the right hand of the throne of God.
Hebrews 12:1-2

This passage in Hebrews encourages Christians to run the race that is set before us with perseverance. Many Christians in the early centuries did run the race and like Jesus were executed. They were martyred for their faith. Like Jesus they were looking past the immediate suffering to eternal life. But what of those left behind? The heartache of losing a family member or friend in such a way had to be devastating. Dealing with the loss of someone we love may be the most difficult thing we have to deal with in life. We find it difficult to function. Anger, denial, loss of purpose, extreme sadness, hopelessness plague us. As we persevere in this grueling race of grief, we feel like we take up our cross daily.

The Hardest Thing

What was the hardest
Thing you have done?
Run a marathon?
Lose a son?

43

You may limp for a few days
After running 26.2
But you're crippled for life
After the loss of a child,
Loss of a spouse,
Loss.

You may crumple in exhaustion
After you cross the finish line
Because you pushed your body
Beyond what is normal.
You asked more than
Your body could give.
But it did.

The marathon of grief
Is run on many courses,
Loss of a Child Ultra
Losing a Spouse Endurance Run
Sibling Loss Triathlon
Death of a Parent Challenge
Losing a Friend Marathon.

All sap your strength.
All carry you beyond
What you can do.
The finish line
Never appears.
You are never done.

The running never stops
Like an ultramarathon
Without an end
On and on and on
Day after day.

Your pace varies.
Sometimes you sprint

So that you don't have to feel
The emotions.

Other days you crawl
Because you cannot even
Make it to your feet.

Sometimes you trip
Fall down
Get up
Only to stumble
And fall again.

The best days you run
With a friend
Matching your stride
Sharing the road of grief.

The hardest runs find you
All alone
Running in
Desolation
Tears falling
With each step.

Stride for stride
Your broken heart keeps
Pumping through the pain.
Everything hurts.

Every fiber of your being
Wants to stop
To quit this race
But there is nothing else
No other life now
Than to run
The race of grief.

Tethered to death

Who goes before you.
You cannot stop.
You cannot resist
You are pulled along
Even dragged
If you refuse
To run.

There is no escape.

So you press on
Compelled to take
Another step
Another stabbing heartbeat,
A stream of tears,
Blistered,
Battered souls,
There is no end.

Up until the death of my son, the hardest thing I had done was to speak at my sister's funeral and endure losing her. I felt such an overwhelming pain and sadness. I just wanted to run away rather than step up to the podium. My heart was breaking and the words barely came out.

Since then I've spoken at the funerals of my father-in-law, my mother-in-law, the memorials of both my brothers-in-law. Not only speaking at the services but also dealing with those deaths has been very difficult.

But when my son died, I could not speak at his service. I wrote several pages about my son that a friend read. Enduring that day and the days since have been most difficult.

Encouragement

Facing the death of a loved one is one of the most difficult things we do as humans. Working through the grief after such a loss takes everything out of us. How do you get through it? Any way you can. Yes, you can. Although it may be the most difficult thing that you have ever done, you will get through this. You may want to quit, throw in the towel, but you have to keep putting one foot in front of the other to finish the race that you have been forced to run.

Moving Forward

1. If you are unable to cope, check with your physician about medication to help you get through the worst of grief. This may be important for your mental health.

2. Sleep is important. If sleep eludes you and over-the-counter medications do not help, check with your physician.

3. Read and reflect on Psalm 59.

Prayer

God of grace, help us as we stumble through this grief. Give us strength to go on, when all we want to do is to stop. When sleep is impossible and rest eludes us, grant us your peace and calm. Heal our brokenness so that we can carry on with life. Let us know you are with us as we limp along in pain. You always give us hope. Amen.

9 Compounding Griefs

When Jacob ended his charge to his sons, he drew up his feet into the bed, breathed his last, and was gathered to his people. Then Joseph threw himself on his father's face and wept over him and kissed him. Joseph commanded the physicians in his service to embalm his father. So the physicians embalmed Israel; they spent forty days in doing this, for that is the time required for embalming. And the Egyptians wept for him seventy days.
Genesis 49:33-50:3

Six months into the grief of my son I remembered another grief. The day marked the 50th anniversary of the assassination of President Kennedy. I was ten years old at the time. He was buried on my birthday, November 25, 1963, fifty years ago.

My mother had the policy of never allowing us to miss a day of school. However, she would permit us to play hooky on our birthdays. The three channels we had on television only carried news coverage of the state funeral all day long. I remember it being a sad and boring day for a now 11-year-old, whose siblings and friends were in school. It was a day I could not understand. It marked the beginning of an education in violent death--Robert Kennedy, Martin Luther King, Jr., Vietnam, violent protests, and police retaliation—and the beginning of an education in loss.

A Boy and a Horse

Fifty years ago today,

48

They laid to rest a young president,
On my 11th birthday.

Got to stay home that day.
Some birthday celebration!
Black and white covered,
The state funeral all day long.

No friends or siblings.
All at school in hushed classrooms.
Only somber tones,
Tearful faces.

JFK to LBJ.
What difference to me?
Just a kid.
Innocence gone.

I saw the black horse
In the parade.
They called him "Black Jack"
What would he say today?

"More than 1,000 times
I have borne the weight
Of the dead

Of JFK
And LBJ
And a thousand others

Carrying only the saddle
With empty boots reversed in the stirrups
To represent my fallen, invisible rider.

A 'riderless horse'
They call me
Following the flag-draped
Casket in the parade

But I carry the weight
Of the grief of a nation
The burden of an aching absence

Who can weigh the
Emptiness who rides me?
Would a hundred million tears
Balance the scale?"

Black Jack's cremated ashes buried
In 1976, the year I got married.
Full military honors for a horse
Who bore the compounding griefs
Of a nation.

When we suffer the loss of a loved one, all our previous losses are rekindled. Grief brings in reinforcements as you remember the pain of the past. My sister's death, my father-in-law's three years later. My brother-in-law's suicide. My mother-in-law passed after suffering for years with Alzheimer's. Other griefs come to bear witness that the pain of other losses is not gone, not healed, not completely. I am learning that you must re-live some of those scenes as you work through grief again.

Encouragement
It's normal to think about other deaths that you have experienced as you bear the fresh pain of grief. It does not mean you are crazy or morbid. Grief naturally connects those experiences in our minds. It is part of the process. Remembering other losses does add to the sadness as you think about how you loved them. Your feelings come back to you from the distant past. The burden of the current loss becomes even heavier. Even though you may question how you are going to make it, remember that you did get through grief in the past. You will get through this difficult time as well.

Moving Forward

1. Rather than avoid thinking about the death of your loved ones, when you are ready, make a list of those you have lost. Write by each name why they were important to you, what you miss most about them, what you liked best about them. Offer a prayer of thanks for each as you remember your relationship with them and how they touched your life.

2. Read and reflect on Psalm 130.

Prayer

For all those we have loved and lost, we grieve, O Lord. Be near us as the burden is compounded with another loss. Comfort us, as only you can! Amen.

10 All Gone!

*They will fly away like a dream, and not be found;
they will be chased away like a vision of the night.
The eye that saw them will see them no more,
nor will their place behold them any longer.*

*Their bodies, once full of youth,
will lie down in the dust with them.*
Job 20:8-9, 11

Absence does not make the heart grow fonder. The death of one we love shatters our hearts. Their absence drives us deep into grief and mourning.

"All Gone!"

Death stops
Our plans,
Trumps our future,
Kills off hope
For a better day,
For a new tomorrow.

He spoke of
Going
Back to school.

She talked with
Glee about
Their upcoming
Wedding.

They planned the
European vacation
To celebrate
His retirement.

She had decided
To take
That exciting
New job.

They were
Talking about
Names for
The baby.

About to
Move into their
New home . . .

Our dreams crash
Like crystal falling out
Of our hands
Shattering into
A thousand pieces
At our feet.

With my son's death
His hopes have died.
His plans for his business,
For further education
Breathe no more.

His dream
Of sailing

Around the world,
Of visiting
Different peoples
And countries,
Plunged into
Murky depths
Down into
The black abyss.

His goals to understand,
To read all the books
He could,
To delve deeper
Into philosophy,
Asking the
Hard questions
That stretch the mind,
Have snapped like a flimsy
Rubber band.

His creative brilliance
His flashes of insight
Have been silenced
Forever.

His push to be financially secure
From his meager beginnings,
Cut off before he could
Be established.

His rocky relationship
With his girlfriend
Will never be restored.

Death brings a dead end
To all that could be.
No outlet for his hopes
No future for his dreams

The line has stopped.
No children
No grandchildren
No play, or giggles
Or glee.

"All gone!" is what
We said when he
Had finished
The jar of baby food
As he sat in his high chair.

"All gone!"
Is all we can say
Now.

My wife experienced physical pain in the center of her chest after our son died. I was worried about her. When talking with a man who lost his daughter two months later, he was also experiencing an ache in the middle of his chest. This physical symptom must be where the idea of having a broken heart comes from. While there may not be permanent damage to our physical hearts, our emotional scars never heal completely. At the root of this physical and emotional pain is our loss. We would never speak to him again.

Even though the motels were booked and the plane tickets purchased for our vacation together with him, he was gone. We cancelled the motel reservations. We kept the plane tickets so that we could go to California to pick up his ashes, see the home he had recently purchased and grieve with his girlfriend and his best friend. We got all his friends and fellow motorcycle couriers together at his house. Many of them rode their motorcycles an hour and a half to get there. When they parked side by side down the street, they left an empty space for our son's motorcycle. We all shared memories. But he was gone. Nothing can replace one you love. There will always be a gaping hole in the middle of our hearts.

Encouragement

Intense sadness comes with grief. Absence brings pain. A thousand triggers remind us of our loss--an empty chair, a photo, a stranger whose hair reminds us of her, his favorite song. They reinforce our feelings of depression. Absence shatters our hearts. It's normal for you to feel deep sadness.

You may feel overwhelmed long after the loss. Is there any encouragement? Eventually you will be able to deal with the sadness more easily. No, life will never be the same. The absence will always be painful, but with time you can adjust to this new reality and learn to bear this grief. It may take a long time, but you will feel better.

Moving Forward

1. Talk with those who knew the one you lost. Share stories, photographs and memories of her or him.

2. Read aloud the following lines from Psalm 23 (1-4) several times today.

The LORD is my shepherd, I shall not want.
He makes me lie down in green pastures;
he leads me beside still waters;
he restores my soul.
He leads me in right paths
for his name's sake.
Even though I walk through the darkest valley,
I fear no evil;
for you are with me;
your rod and your staff —
they comfort me.

Prayer

Lord, we feel so deeply their absence. The pain of not being able to be with the one we lost, tears us apart inside. Help us to live with the gaping hole in the middle of our hearts. Empower us to live through the sadness. Amen.

ANGER AND GUILT

11 Damn you, Death!

For my soul is full of troubles,
and my life draws near to Sheol.
I am counted among those who go down to the Pit;
I am like those who have no help,
like those forsaken among the dead,
like the slain that lie in the grave,
like those whom you remember no more,
for they are cut off from your hand.
You have put me in the depths of the Pit,
in the regions dark and deep.
Your wrath lies heavy upon me,
and you overwhelm me with all your waves.
Psalm 88:3-7

A young woman had a tonsillectomy and went home. The next day her father found her in her room. She had bled out. From a tonsillectomy? Damn you, Death!

A 21-year-old was to have a minor procedure for which she needed general anesthesia. She never came out. She died on the operating table. The parents were so devastated they never came back to church—angry with God. Damn you, Death!

Even though the nursery is finished, the obstetrician says there is no heartbeat. Damn you, Death!

Parents watch as their son battles cancer, tortured daily by the disease. He loses his fight. Damn you, Death!

We are angry when we lose someone we love. We are angry with God, doctors, cancer, heart disease, dementia, the blood clot, the drunk driver, the murderer, the police officers, the enemy soldier. . . . We are angry at death. We are even angry with ourselves that we could not do something to stop death from taking our loved ones.

Damn you, Death!

Damn you, Death!

Unjust judge!
You condemn
Without trial or
Hearing.

You blindside
Parents of babies
Stealing the little one
Most precious to them,
Taking away their
Reason to live.

You kidnap parents
Whose children must wander
Without their guardians
Who cared most about them.

You take graduates
Full of promise.
You take brides
Who had given theirs.

You take the weak.
You take the strong.
You take the sick.

58

You take the healthy.
You take the young.
You take the old.

You take, take, take . . . .

You never give back.

You take by surprise.
Suddenly without warning.
A crash
A clot
A shot

You torture with slow agonizing pain.
Cell by cell the cancer spreads.
The dementia cripples
One synapse after another.

Bully Death,
You taunt us,
Beat us,
Torture us,
Crush us.

You are stronger.
We cannot resist.
You are faster.
We cannot get away.

We are helpless
Like injured field mice
In the playful paws
Of a Siberian tiger.

We are nothing to you,
Only something to devour,
Plankton for the whale,
Fodder for the cow,

Chum for the shark.

Curse you, Death!

Damned you are!
All your terrors
Undone in the
Resurrection
Of the Son!

Doomed you are!
Our distant hope
Rested on the lips
Of martyrs whom
You burned alive,
Tortured on crosses.

Their silence
Echoes through the ages:
"Death will be no more!"
Damn you, Death.
And so you are.

Pastors are not supposed to get angry. Yet I am angry with God for not protecting my son. I am angry with the other driver who likely caused my son to crash. I am even angry with my son for not taking the train into Los Angeles instead of riding his motorcycle. I am angry with myself for not convincing him to do so. I am angry with death, whose work I have seen far too often. I am learning that anger is a normal part of grief. It's okay to be angry.

Encouragement

Grief stirs up anger in us. Don't apologize for feeling angry. It is better if you can control your anger so that you don't lash out at those around you, who may also be dealing with grief. But if you go on the attack, cut yourself some slack. Understand that your emotions are raw when you grieve.

Moving Forward

1. The Apostle Paul says that ultimately death will lose because of Christ. He points to the resurrection of our bodies and the victory that will come. This hope may not banish our anger or evaporate our sadness. However, in time hope may comfort us. Reflect on the following passage:

> *When this perishable body puts on imperishability, and this mortal body puts on immortality, then the saying that is written will be fulfilled:*
> *"Death has been swallowed up in victory."*
> *"Where, O death, is your victory?*
> *Where, O death, is your sting?"*
>
> *The sting of death is sin, and the power of sin is the law. But thanks be to God, who gives us the victory through our Lord Jesus Christ. Therefore, my beloved, be steadfast, immovable, always excelling in the work of the Lord, because you know that in the Lord your labor is not in vain.* (1 Corinthians 15:54-58)

2. Reflect on the following questions:

- Can I accept the fact that I am angry? Am I okay with that?
- What is the focus of my anger in this moment?
- How have I been able to control my anger?
- When I have lost control, what have the consequences been?
- How can I express my anger in healthy ways?

Prayer

Lord, we acknowledge these feelings of anger. They are not wrong. You have created us as emotional beings. Our emotions are raw in grief. When we are angry, help us not to judge ourselves as bad people because of our anger. Help us to feel the anger and to control the rage within so that we do not harm ourselves or others. May we know your grace even in the midst of our anger. May the hope of your victory over death take over our rage and grant us peace. Amen.

12 Angry with God

Jesus told his friends, "Are not two sparrows sold for a penny? Yet not one of them will fall to the ground apart from your Father. And even the hairs of your head are all counted. So do not be afraid; you are of more value than many sparrows."
Matthew 10:29-31

What are we worth to God? More than many sparrows. That's a relief. But how many?

How many pennies are we worth in God's economy? When we lose someone we love, we ask if God cared at all. Why did he or she have to die? Wasn't God able to do something to stop it, to bring healing, to prevent the accident? Don't we believe in a God who is powerful and caring? Or is God just idly standing by?

In the above verses Jesus is speaking about the fear of death. He says that we don't have to worry. "Do not fear those who kill the body but cannot kill the soul; rather fear him who can destroy both soul and body in hell."

In other words, if you want to fear someone, fear God. Jesus seems to be acknowledging that evil people might kill the disciples, but they should not worry about that because God knows. God cares and is aware of us, even our hair count, at all times and in all places. In the end the most evil people can do is kill your body.

But God has control over your body and your soul. Jesus is pointing to the Eternal and Infinite in a world of sparrows and thinning hair. Jesus is giving us hope that God cares now and forever. We should know that his care for us is real and runs beyond this reality even when death comes, especially when death comes.

My Bystander God

So You know when a little bird dies?
Then I have no need to furnish
His obituary,
Information you already have
And much more.
You knew the number of hairs
Inside that helmet
Which did not save him.

Neither did you, O Lord,
My Bystander God.

Perhaps it's not fair
To think so little of you.
All I can hope
Is that you were there,
That he was not alone
That now he is there with you.

Was it like with Job?
Had you wagered with Satan
Who went too far and took his life?
No innocent bystander is my God.
He could have done something to stop it.

Am I so ungrateful for all those times
When he could have died
But did not?
I always gave thanks to you
For watching out for him.

63

But this time
Were you just
Watching?

We call you "Heavenly Father"
But are you just a deadbeat Dad
Who abandons
His children
Especially when they need something?

Forgive me
For judging you
For doubting you
For being angry with you.

Help me to understand,
God of love
Omnipotent
Omniscient
Omnipresent
How you could let him die?

I am learning it is okay to be angry with God—even for a pastor. Job was angry with God. Jeremiah was angry with God. Neither of them was punished for being angry with the Lord. God can take our anger. When we love someone, and they are taken from us, it is natural to wonder, "Where was God? Why didn't God do something?"

I believe there is no sin in communicating that to God. The sin comes when we walk away from God, turning our backs on God. Of course, our anger can lead to our walking away.

The good news? God will always welcome us with open arms if we return. I believe that God would rather hear me insulting him in my anger than see my back as I turn away from him in bitterness. God would rather I be honest in my pain than abandon my faith.

Encouragement

Don't give up on yourself even if you find some attitudes and thoughts in your own mind that are not what you would hope to find in a person of faith. Being angry with God, or even just disappointed in the Almighty, is natural in a time like this. It is common for someone who is grieving to doubt God's love (Doesn't God care?) or God's power (Couldn't God have done something?). It's okay to entertain such thoughts. In fact, I would wonder if you are being honest if you do not have such thoughts.

Moving Forward

1. Read Job, chapter 7. Note how Job complains against God's injustice.

2. Take some time to tell God how you really feel—even if it's ugly. Write it out if you want. You can destroy it later. Just express yourself for now.

Prayer

We confess that in our anger, Lord, we doubted your love for us and for the ones we love. We thought of you as doing nothing, like a guilty bystander. We concluded you had abandoned us, like a deadbeat dad. Yet we know you stand by us at all times, even when things have gone wrong, even when we are wrong. Forgive us for not respecting you in our anger. Thank you for being there for us and for the ones we have lost. We are grateful that you are always with us. We are never alone. You always care even if we don't understand all that has happened. Grant us the confidence in you, in your love and power in all places and at all times, even now. Amen.

13 Surely not I, Lord?

When it was evening, he took his place with the twelve; and while they were eating, he said, "Truly I tell you, one of you will betray me." And they became greatly distressed and began to say to him one after another, "Surely not I, Lord?" He answered, "The one who has dipped his hand into the bowl with me will betray me. The Son of Man goes as it is written of him, but woe to that one by whom the Son of Man is betrayed! It would have been better for that one not to have been born." Judas, who betrayed him, said, "Surely not I, Rabbi?" He replied, "You have said so."
Matthew 26:20-25

A few months before our son died, one of my wife Yvonne's Sunday school children lost her baby sister, who was just a year old. A few weeks after Samuel died, our neighbor across the street, who had been so compassionate to both of us in our loss, died suddenly, working out at the gym. He was only 60. Two weeks later our nursery worker had a tonsillectomy and inexplicably bled as she slept. She was 34. Yvonne was her supervisor and friend. As we neared the first anniversary of our son's death, our youth worker's baby died in utero. Three days before the anniversary of our son's death, friends of ours in the church lost their son, 39 years old.

Six days after the anniversary of our son's death, Yvonne's sister's son Matt died in his sleep at 36 years old. It was totally unexpected! As we were coming home from Matt's service in South Carolina, our best friends called to let us know their son died, having lost his battle with cancer. Five weeks later on our son's birthday, July 21, a good friend of ours in the church lost her son suddenly. He was 36. He also died in his sleep.

In light of these premature and unexpected deaths, all closely connected to us, Yvonne was told, "It does not pay to be your friend." Although it sounds cruel, it was not intended that way. Nor did Yvonne take it that way. But she was already thinking it herself. We both were. "Is it I, Lord? Is there some kind of curse on us? What have we done wrong? Do people need to keep away from us—not get close to us?"

Some did seem to pull away from us. Maybe they were frightened. Sometimes you wonder when several losses pile up on you if you are to blame. It sounds completely superstitious. But you start to wonder anyway. For all our intelligence, sometimes emotions trump logic.

When Jesus said that one of the twelve would betray him, they all started asking, "Surely not I, Lord?" They questioned him while questioning themselves. Will I be at fault? Will I let him down?

When death comes, the questions flood the mind. "Did I do wrong?" "Am I to blame?" "If only I had done . . . , then they would not have died." Guilt is one of the most common feelings to plague us as we grieve. "Surely not I, Lord?"

Guilty on All Counts!

It's my fault.
I did it.
Guilty as charged.
Loud and clear
My confession
Rings out
In the courtroom
Of my mind.

Again and again
I am convicted

67

Sentenced to life
Without parole.

I am judge and jury,
A speedy trial
Because I know
It was I.

But the cross examination
Goes on and on
Long after the verdict.

Why didn't I . . .
How could I . . .
If only I . . .
I shouldn't have . . .
What kind of father . . .
Surely I am to blame for . . .
Why wasn't I there to . . .
Wasn't it I, who . . .

Cast into
The dungeon of darkness
I weep on the dirt floor
Turning it into mud.

I call for them
To drag me
To the wooden rack
I command to be bound
And stretched
"Turn the spindles
one more notch!"

Tossed back onto
The muddy floor
The accusations
Begin again
As I regain consciousness.

It was you!
It's your fault!
Guilty as charged!
He'd be alive if only
You had . . .

Day after day
Verdict and sentence
Trial and torture

Until rumbling from
Deep within my soul
I cry out,
Echoing the agony of St. Paul,
"Wretched man that I am!
Who will rescue me
From this body of death?"

The heavy door creaks open
Light floods my guilty cell
A voice announces
"In Christ there is
No condemnation.
You are free to go."

But will I?
Can I?
Must I?

I have learned that while guilt is a normal part of grieving, it adds to the overwhelming shock and sadness. When people compound the guilt by pointing the finger at you, they are only confirming what you already feel, which does not help. Eventually reason and the grace of God helped me get through the emotions that filled me with negative and untrue thoughts. I was not to blame—no matter what I was saying to myself or what others were saying. Certainly I had made many mistakes as a father. God's grace has been present in my life as I continue to work through the guilt of grief. Yes, there are still moments I feel guilty. But I can set these feelings aside much more easily now. In other words, I am learning to forgive myself and let go of the guilt.

Encouragement

It's pointless for me or anyone to say to you, "Don't feel guilty." Guilt is something that most people wrestle with even though there is no logical reason for it. But what if there is? What if you somehow caused your loved one's death? I believe that even if that is the case, you can learn to forgive yourself.

Jesus said from the cross, "Father forgive them, for they do not know what they are doing." Who was he asking God to forgive? The soldiers who were crucifying him? The crowd who had demanded his execution? The religious leaders? Pilate? Judas?

Yes, all of the above. God will forgive us of all of our sins if we ask. God's grace will help us learn to forgive ourselves. It may take some time, but it can happen. We can let go of the guilt. We can be free.

Moving Forward

1. Talk about your feelings of guilt with a trained counselor or pastor.

2. Though it may be difficult, write a list what you wish you had done differently. At the end of the list, write a letter to your loved one asking for his or her forgiveness.

3. Reflect on the question: If Jesus forgave those who crucified him, wouldn't the Lord forgive me?

4. Read and reflect on Psalm 51.

Prayer

God of grace and mercy, reveal your love to those of us who struggle with guilt over the loss of our loved ones. Forgive us and help us to feel the assurance that you are not holding anything against us. Help us to let go of what we are holding against ourselves. Set us free from guilt by your grace. Amen.

14 Guilty!

I do not understand my own actions. For I do not do what I want, but I do the very thing I hate. Now if I do what I do not want, I agree that the law is good. But in fact it is no longer I that do it, but sin that dwells within me. For I know that nothing good dwells within me, that is, in my flesh. I can will what is right, but I cannot do it. For I do not do the good I want, but the evil I do not want is what I do. Now if I do what I do not want, it is no longer I that do it, but sin that dwells within me.

So I find it to be a law that when I want to do what is good, evil lies close at hand. For I delight in the law of God in my inmost self, but I see in my members another law at war with the law of my mind, making me captive to the law of sin that dwells in my members. Wretched man that I am! Who will rescue me from this body of death? Thanks be to God through Jesus Christ our Lord!
Romans 7:15-25

Paul reveals the struggle all of us have. We all do things we regret. We are unloving at times. We are hurtful to others at times. The Law says, "Love your neighbor as yourself!" (Lev. 19:18). Yet we often only love ourselves. Sometimes we ignore or harbor resentment against our neighbor. So what do we do with our failures? How do we find the help we need to love others?

Paul says in Romans 7:25, "Thanks be to God through Jesus Christ our Lord!" Then he launches into an explanation of his ultimate discovery for Christians--Romans 8:1. "There is therefore now no condemnation for those who are in Christ Jesus."

No condemnation? We have all messed up. How can we not be condemned for our sins? Paul says that the judgment against us is dismissed because of grace. Faith in Christ has brought the gift of God's grace to us. Even our faith is a gift of grace.

Guilty!

Guilty!
That's the verdict
That keeps echoing through my mind.
Bad Dad!
Impatient!

Cared more about his job than his son.
Exploded with anger on many occasions.
Broken promises to a little boy.
How could you?

Guilt erases the memory of mercy
Of forgiveness, of reconciliation.
When I wonder if that's what really happened,
If there wasn't more to the story,
Guilt screams at me.

Guilt perverts justice
Bribes the judge
In the courtroom of my mind.
The light bulb hangs over my head.
I am tied to the chair.

"Cats in the Cradle" blares
Over and over and over.
"When you coming home, Dad?"
"I don't know when,
But we'll get together then, son.
We're going to have a good time, then!"

My attorney for the defense is absent.
Yet the trial goes on.
Hot tears flow down my cheeks.
I await the sentencing
Which can only be
"Life without the possibility of parole"

Forever to wear the
Electronic ankle bracelet
Of Regret
Which goes off whenever
I make
A run toward Grace.

Forever to be buried alive
With just enough air to gasp
For Mercy, which has been told,
"He's gone. It's too late."

In my grief I need grace more than ever. I need to know my sins are forgiven. In some of my conversations with my son, I had the distinct impression that he had forgiven me for messing up as a father. But we never really talked it out fully. When I mentioned how I thought we had been too strict at times, his reply was, "I think you should have been even more strict." Perhaps he did not condemn my parenting mistakes. We definitely needed to talk more about that for his sake and mine. We did not have that opportunity. He is gone. But God's grace is not.

Encouragement
In the midst of the pain of grief is guilt. As with the other emotions, sometimes it is in the background; other times it is overwhelming and brings tears to our eyes. Why could I have not been a better parent, a better husband or wife, a better son or daughter, sister, brother, friend?

Guilt is the flashing neon sign with the pointing finger: Bad! Bad! Bad! The loudspeaker blares messages like: Why weren't you more patient with him? Why didn't you love her more? Why didn't you pay more attention to her instead of your work? Why weren't you there for him?

The problem with guilt is that it has the evidence to convict you in the courtroom of your mind. Those memories are real. But only part of the evidence is presented. It leaves out the scenes of forgiveness and acceptance, of relationships restored. The prosecution omits the happy times.

There is no grace in this kind of guilt. It only piles on the guilty verdicts so that the only outcome can be a string of life sentences—sentenced to feel like a failure, sentenced always to feel bad. But guilt only uses part of the story, half-truths to bury the living. As you feel guilty, allow yourself the freedom to remember what you did well, the good in your relationship. There was much good despite what your guilt tells you. Turn to God's amazing grace.

Moving Forward

1. Paul follows up the above passage by writing with a sense of peace and freedom. Read and reflect on this passage:

> *There is therefore now no condemnation for those who are in Christ Jesus. For the law of the Spirit of life in Christ Jesus has set you free from the law of sin and of death.* (Romans 8:1-2)

2. Find a copy of "Amazing Grace." Sing or read the words aloud.

Prayer

Most loving God, if you were to hold our sins against us, who would survive? Yet you have offered us grace, which we desperately need. You have promised us mercy and pardon of sins. May your grace be real in our lives and in the lives of all who feel guilt over what cannot be undone! Please rescue us from the guilt, which reverberates in the chambers of our hearts and in the courtrooms of our minds. Amen.

15 I Was Not There

Meanwhile, standing near the cross of Jesus were his mother, and his mother's sister, Mary the wife of Clopas, and Mary Magdalene.
John 19:25

Mary stood at the foot of the cross when Jesus was crucified. Her sister and other women were there at her side. Jesus' friend John stood by them. How did they say, "Goodbye"? What do you say at the execution of one you love? Can you speak at all? I cannot imagine anything more difficult.

A woman approached me before the worship service, it was the first time I had seen her since her mother passed away. I expressed my condolences. She told me her cousins were angry with her because she did not make it to the hospital in time. When she found out her mother, who had Alzheimer's, was admitted to the hospital, she had reserved a cross-country flight for the next day the earliest available. Her brother did the same from overseas. However, their mother passed before either of them could get there. Their cousins were not speaking to them because they were not with their mother before she died. I asked if the cousins were there. She said they were. I tried to console her both for the loss of her mother and for being the target of her cousins' anger.

As a pastor people often tell me how their loved one died. They tell me if they were in the hospital room by the bed when he or she passed away. Sometimes all the family is there in that final moment. People share the guilt of not having made it home. Others sob as they say they had just stepped out of the room for a few moments when he died. They were not there in the final moment. Some talk about giving permission for her to die, and how she slipped away. Does having that chance to say "Goodbye" make it any easier? Would words have helped? Many people do not get the chance to say "Goodbye." Perhaps being there at the end does not make it any easier at all.

I Was Not There

The least I could have done
Was to be there
With you when
You died.

A father should do that
For a son.

But I was not there
To hold your hand
Or to comfort you.

They said you died
On impact
Died alone
Before the paramedics
Could get there,
Died
Before anyone
Could help.

I am sorry I was not there
With you when you
Left this world.

A father should be there
For his son.

I was there when you
Were born,
Took your first
Breath, even
Got to hold you
First.

I was there when you
Learned to walk
Spoke your first words
Learned to drive
Got your first car
Entered drug treatment
Got clean
Enrolled in college.

But not at the end.
Not at the most important
Moment.

As your Dad
I should have been there
For you.

I am sorry
You died alone.
I was not there
To remind you
How much I
Love you
How much your
Mom, sister, grandma,
Grandpa . . .
All love you.

Would it have helped
To have placed my
Breaking heart
By your broken

Body,
To have held you
As your breathed
Your last,
To have done
Mouth-to-mouth
Or CPR?

Would I have held your hand,
Something we had not done
Since you were little?

Would that have added
Discomfort to your pain?
Perhaps you would not want
Me to see you like that,
Bloody and broken.

Could I have done it?
Could I have held you
In my arms
As your heart stopped
Beating
As your eyes went
Blank?
Would I?

Sons leave
Fly their own skies
Sail their own seas
Ride their own
Canyon roads
Die alone.

If I had an opportunity to talk with my son as he lay dying by the side of the road, what would I have said? Yes, I would have said, "I love you more than I can say. I am proud of you. Even with all the conflict we've had through the years, I am happy you were my son." "I am sorry for the pain that I caused you."

78

"Forgive me for not being a better dad." "I am sorry for not being home more to be with you, for working 70+ hours a week most of your life." Had I known it was going to be our last conversation the day before he died, what would I have said to him? I know I would not have ended our conversation to be on time for my meeting. I would have conversed with him through the day and night. I know I would have affirmed my love for him and his importance to me—certainly more than I did. Although it sounds trite, I've learned we can't go back or change the past. Even though we can think of a thousand better endings, we can't re-write the story. It's the one that has been written for us.

Encouragement

We never want to let go of a loved one. You may have wanted it to be different at the end. If you did not get a chance for a final time together at the end of their life, that is certainly part of your loss. On the other hand, if you had to watch as they suffered until the final moment, like Mary at the cross of Jesus, that painful memory is part of your sorrow. Whether you were informed by military officers at your door, or by a coroner's phone call, or you watched them breathe their last, those moments are carved in the stone of your memory. You can learn to live with that part of the pain. Over time you will come to accept your presence or absence as part of your grief journey. Your sense of guilt will subside. If others harbor anger or disappointment against you, I hope that will fade quickly and that you may be reconciled.

Moving Forward

1. If you did not have a chance to speak with you loved one when they died, write what you would have wanted your conversation to be or go into a room by yourself and tell them what you would have said.

2. If you were with your loved one at the end, write down what you said to them. Describe feelings you remember. If they did speak, write down what they said.

3. As you work through your grief, repeat the prayer, "God be merciful to me a sinner," whenever guilt and regrets assail.

4. Read and reflect on Psalm 32.

Prayer

Lord, bless all of us who did not have a chance to say, "Goodbye." Our loved one was taken with no opportunity for a final word, a final embrace, a last kiss. Comfort all those who were there and endured the pain of watching as the one they loved slipped from this life. Give us comfort, courage and strength to face what happened and to live with the loss. Help us to reconcile with family and friends. Give us faith to believe that though our time together has ended here, we will be together in eternity. Fill us with hope that our "Goodbye" may mean "Until we meet again." Amen.

FRIENDS AND MEMORIES

16 One-Line Fixes

Think now, who that was innocent ever perished?
Or where were the upright cut off?"
As I have seen, those who plow iniquity
and sow trouble reap the same.
Job 4:7-8

As for me, I would seek God,
and to God I would commit my cause.
Job 5:8

These words were spoken by Job's friend Eliphaz from Teman. Job, a righteous man, had suffered tremendous loss. All his children had been killed. He had lost all his wealth, measured in livestock in those days. On top of that he had been afflicted with terrible sores all over his body. After sitting in silence with Job and his other two friends for a week, Eliphaz finally spoke. He would have been a better friend had he remained silent. First, Eliphaz told Job that innocent people do not suffer, only the wicked. Then he suggested that Job seek God. Job had been seeking and would continue to seek God for the trials that had come upon him, which he did not deserve. Eliphaz attempted an explanation of Job's predicament, pointing the finger at Job. He was trying to provide an easy answer to Job's suffering. He wanted to fix the situation by giving his advice. Not helpful.

The week my wife and I began language training as missionaries in Brazil, the father of one of our language school teachers died suddenly. At that time in Brazil most burials took place within 24 hours of death. So all of us from the language school went to the funeral the next morning. None of us could say anything in Portuguese except "Good morning. How are you?" We were anxious to know what to say. So the teachers taught us the Portuguese phrase, "meus pesames," meaning "my condolences".

All of us missionary pastors and professors shook hands with the grieving family and said practically the only words we knew in Portuguese—"meus pesames." We might have wanted to say more, but we had no vocabulary. It turned out that was enough. When someone experiences a loss, we want to say something to make the person feel better. The truth is that nothing we say is going to make their grief less painful. As one pastoral care professor told us ministerial students, "There are no magic words to take their pain away. However, there are things you should not say."

People mean well when they say things like, "Time Heals All Wounds" and other platitudes. They just don't know what to say. Usually the less said, the better. I had my fill of one-line fixes the day after my son died. Sometimes these one-line wonders made me angry. We live in a world of sound bytes, of quick fixes, of instant everything. It is understandable people want to give you a one-liner to help you in your anguish--inappropriate, but understandable.

One-line Fixes for My Broken Heart

"At least you have your memories!"
Is this one-line drug
Supposed to heal my heart?
Is this meant to assuage
My pain?
Do you really think
That helps?

82

"It was God's will."
This one-line wonder
Tops the charts
Of pat answers.
No music there
To soothe my soul

How can a good God
Will a death?
From cancer to crashes,
From cardiac arrests
To shootings at point
Blank range,
From tornadoes
To tonsillectomies bled out. . .

Does God orchestrate
All this pain and loss?
Even if God is to blame,
How does that help
Me carry this pain?

"God needed another angel for the choir."
Do people drop out of
God's choir?
That they need to be replaced?
Do they get mad at the Director?

Are we to envision a
Malevolent Maestro
Or a diabolical Diva
Who insists on
Another voice
To back her melody.

Is this a Kidnapper God
Who steals a child
For such a paltry purpose?

83

"At least you have another child."
May this shallow line
Be buried in a shallow grave
Never to be spoken again!

Would you tell the man
Who just had his right arm
Ripped out of its socket,
"At least you have your left"?
Wouldn't you instead
Try to stop
The bleeding?!

"Time heals all wounds"
Time may also make me
Crazy with grief.

Time makes things
Rust and decay,
Rot and putrify.
Time discards
As obsolete.
Time sidelines
As no longer relevant.
Time brings dementia
And atrophy.

What fool assumes
That time
Is on his side,
Positing a benevolence
Of minutes and seconds
Which may be
Merely the ticking
Countdown
To an unexpected
Explosion.

Tell the diabetic
Amputee that times
Heals all wounds.

Tell the addict
Who struggles to be free
That time
Heals all wounds.

"Let it go and move on."
How can I let go of my son?
Wouldn't that be letting go of
Love?
Letting go of who I am as
His father?

"Get over it."
As if grief were only
A little knoll
To be easily
Conquered.
So quickly spoken
Only by those who have
Never faced Everest.

"Have faith!"
Does my grief imply
I do not believe?
Or is it we believers
Have perfected the art
Of kicking a person
When he is down?

You deal these cheap
Street drugs
These one-line fixes.
They cost you nothing
But rip open the wound
Of a grieving parent

85

Who has lost a son.

What is your profit
In dealing these ongoing opiates?
None I can see
Except that you do not
Have to listen to me.

Now I get it!
You are not a
Dealer of the one-line drug
But yourself an addict.

One-line fixes
Your drug of choice
So that you do not have
To feel my pain.

Pat answers
Numb you from feeling
The pain of those
Around you.
Simple one-line anesthetic
Turns you heart to stone.

I am left bleeding on the
Side of the road
As the priest of
Pat answers
Passes by.

"Be strong" was one of the first offenders for me. Does that mean you think I'm not being strong? Do you mean if I cry, I am not strong? If that is what was intended, it was a stupid statement because normal humans cry when they grieve. Does "being strong" mean the same as, "Don't let this grief get to you so that you take own your life." Interpreted that way, it made sense to me. That's how I chose to take it every time someone said, "Be strong" to me. The lesson I am learning is that we all say things that may be inappropriate or insensitive because we don't know what to say. Trying to fix the depth of our brokenness with a one-liner is often offensive.

Encouragement

When people say insensitive or hurtful things, give them the benefit of the doubt and let it go. However, if it is too offensive, tell them so. I did tell a few people that what they said was hurtful or inappropriate. People need to be educated that most grieving people want two things above all else: for their loss to be acknowledged and to be loved. Saying "I am sorry for your loss" or something similar, is all that is needed, especially if it comes from the heart. Being present for someone, as Job's friends did initially, is the best comfort.

Moving Forward

1. Reflect on the following questions:

- What have people said to me that bothered me? What did I reply? What did I want to reply?
- What have I said to others in their time of grief that was probably not helpful?
- What words would be comforting to me?

2. Read and reflect on the following passage from Job 42:7-9. Why would God be angry with Job's friends who constantly defended God, putting the blame on Job?

Prayer

Lord, may the words of our mouths and the meditations of our hearts be acceptable to you as we seek to comfort one another. Amen.

17 Stone Cold Silence

"Their memory perishes from the earth,
and they have no name in the street."
Job 18:17

Bildad, a friend of the suffering Job, is speaking about the fate of the wicked. In ancient Israel there was no belief in an afterlife. The worst that could happen to you was to die with no one to remember you. You only existed in the memory of the ones who loved you and knew you. If no one ever spoke your name after you died, it would be as if you never existed. Your life would have been meaningless.

I Had a Son

You never speak
His name
Or mention
That he lived
And died.

Do you think by
Bringing up his name
Or acknowledging his death
It will make my pain greater?

88

Do you think
Ignoring my loss
Will make my agony
Disappear?

If you never mention his
Name,
Do you think I'll
Forget my pain?

The elephant is in
The room
He's sitting on
My chest.

Pretending this
Burden of grief
Does not exist
Only makes it harder
As I am struggling
For every breath.

You seem to give
More honor to the weather
Or what happened at work
Or the latest baseball standings
Than to my son who lived and died.

Is it that
You do not want to feel sad
So you ignore his life,
His death,
My sorrow?

Your code of silence,
Your pretending,
May protect your feelings
But ignores mine and

Makes you seem
Uncaring, aloof
Above my reality,
No help to me.

It's okay to talk about him,
To remember him,
To laugh at the funny things he did,
To celebrate that he lived,
To mourn that he died
To miss him.

That's what I am doing.

Walk with me in my grief.
Remember with me.
Listen to my stories
As I bear
This load.

That is the only way
You can help
Me carry it.

Do not stroll past
His marker with
Your nose in the air.

Do not trample
His ashes
Under your feet
As if they were not there.

Do not erase
His gravestone
From your heart.

One of the baffling experiences in our loss has been to encounter family members and friends who do not mention our son's name. Their silence has felt to us like they wanted to blot out his memory. They would talk about anything or anyone else except our son, about whom we needed to share memories as part of our grieving.

Scripture teaches us to mourn with those who mourn (Romans 12:15). That means walking with them in their grief. Sometimes it means sitting in silence. Sometimes it means sharing memories of the person who has died. It never means pretending the loss did not happen or that the person never lived.

Encouragement

It's okay to talk about the one you lost, or not talk about them, whichever helps you the most. It does hurt when people, who knew them, will not talk about them with you. Give them permission to share. If they will not, find others who will listen and share their memories about your loved one with you. Do not allow the discomfort of others to stop you from sharing your memories.

Moving Forward

1. Start a journal beginning the opening line on each page with "I remember . . ." Then write down your memories of your loved one.

2. Seek out conversations with people who knew him or her for the purpose of sharing memories.

3. Read and reflect on Psalm 69.

Prayer

Lord, when we comfort others, help us to be good listeners and to be willing to share our stories of the ones they have lost. As we remember our loved ones who have died, help us to find someone with whom we can share those memories — even if it is not the ones we had hoped would share their stories with us. If no one will listen to our stories, allow us to tell them to you. Thank you for remembering, O Lord. Amen.

18 Champions of Grief

And the LORD said to her,
"Two nations are in your womb,
and two peoples born of you shall be divided;
the one shall be stronger than the other,
the elder shall serve the younger."
When her time to give birth was at hand, there were twins in her womb.
The first came out red, all his body like a hairy mantle; so they named
him Esau. Afterward his brother came out, with his hand gripping
Esau's heel.
Genesis 25:23-26

We humans are so competitive. In the story of the first brothers in Genesis, Cain and Abel, Cain becomes jealous of his younger brother and kills him (Genesis 4). Later in Genesis (25) the story is told of Rebekah giving birth to twins Esau and Jacob. Esau is born first, but Jacob comes out grasping Esau's heel, setting up the competition between them throughout their story. The Scripture relates what we all experience in ourselves and with others-- competition. The drive to keep up with and surpass "the Joneses" is not just a modern phenomenon. Competition can have a positive impact in our lives if it spurs us to improve and if we can keep it in balance in our relationships. However, sometimes competition drives us to self-centeredness at the expense of others and alienates those around us. Sometimes we compete even in loss.

Champions of Grief

If I cry more tears
Than you,
Is my grief
More profound?

If you can't stop crying
And cannot
Even work,
Do you win?

How insidious
Our need to outdo
One another
Even
In sorrow!

Friends
Visited us two days
After the death of
Our son.

All they talked about
Was the loss of their
Niece, as if
Their loss was worse.

They needed to talk.
So I listened,
Thinking, "How could you
Bring your little grief
To us when we have
Just lost our son"?

Is it that we want

93

Everyone's attention
Or sympathy?

Like soldiers shouting
Across the battlefield
Hospital tent
"I lost a leg!"
"I can beat that!
I lost both legs!"

Could we measure
Our anguish in limbs lost?
Into how many pieces
Does my heart have to shatter
Before my grief matters
More than yours?

Do we lose points for
The length of time
Elapsed?

Can we work a formula
Combining severity,
Subtracting longevity?

Add 5 points for
Being an eyewitness!
Add 10 for a violent death,
25 for suicide.
Multiply by the inverse
Of the age of the deceased.

Sum up all the deaths
One has experienced.
Double points for those
In the same year,
Triple for the current year.

How foolish we are

To think the depths
Of our human pain
Can be calculated!

Can such personal loss
Be counted an asset
To be compared?
Do we really want
To surpass others
When it comes
To brokenness?

Would it not be better
To cling to one another
Like survivors tossed
By heaving waves
On a stormy sea,
Knowing if we let go of
One another
We will all
Be lost.

Rather than push
Your pain aside
In order to beat you
To that fantasy
Finish line,
Let's stumble together
Picking each other up
As we fall in turn,
Helping,
Healing,
Hoping
To make some progress
Along our path of pain
That has no end.

Recently a man, who lost his wife 18 months ago, told us that our sadness was worse than his because we had lost a child. I assured him that we all suffer in grief. This is not a competition.

I was called to the emergency room at our local hospital. There I met one of our parishioners whose 36-year-old son had just died unexpectedly. She was beside herself with anguish. After I hugged her for several minutes, she dropped back into the metal chair. She looked up at me with tears running down her face and said apologetically, "I am sorry. This is your son's birthday." Surprised she knew that, I responded, "We are all in this together."

That's what I have learned. All who suffer grief travel together on this rocky road. I have found that listening deeply to another's painful story may help them and does me no harm. It does not diminish my loss but helps me connect with someone who is suffering in a similar way. We are bound together in our grief.

Encouragement

People may try to "one-up" your story of sadness with their story. You may be hurt or angry when that happens. Even if you are upset that they are so dismissive of your pain, let them talk. If they are so caught up in their own sorrow that they cannot listen to your pain, pointing that out to them will not help. Just listen. Realize that as much as you may need to be heard, apparently, they do as well. There is a shortage of good listeners.

Moving Forward

1. Find a friend, pastor or counselor, who will listen to your story without competing with you.

2. Practice listening to other's stories of grief without comparing your pain to theirs.

3. Cry out to God and tell God how much you are hurting. God listens.

4. Write about your painful experience. Share what you have written with a friend.

5. Read and reflect on Psalm 143.

Prayer

Lord, let me not compare my grief to another's. Help me not to think their pain is insignificant. Let me not dismiss any who are hurting. Allow me to listen to their pain, giving solace in silence, knowing you care both about their sadness and mine. Amen.

19 Remembering

Still, I think it necessary to send to you Epaphroditus — my brother and co-worker and fellow soldier, your messenger and minister to my need; for he has been longing for all of you, and has been distressed because you heard that he was ill. He was indeed so ill that he nearly died. But God had mercy on him, and not only on him but on me also, so that I would not have one sorrow after another.
Philippians 2:25-27

Paul writes to his friends in Philippi about their mutual friend Epaphroditus, who will deliver this letter to them. Epaphroditus nearly died from an illness but recovered. Paul would have been devastated had Epaphroditus died, as he has suffered the loss of other friends recently.

What is most important in life? When we lose someone we love, what is important becomes painfully and overwhelmingly obvious. It is the people in our lives who matter most. For many of us that means family and close friends. When we lose someone in our inner circle, the loss is unbearable. We want to hang on to them. Suddenly everything about them becomes precious. We may treasure as sacred a keychain or teddy bear. Sooner or later we may have to part with what belonged to them, which brings another loss. Why do these items seem priceless? They connect us to the person we loved and lost. People deal differently with such items. But we cannot let go of our memories. We hang on to them, retelling stories about the one we lost. Yet because we are human and our minds age and change, memories fade.

We used to play a game in our house that my wife Yvonne and my son, Samuel, Jr. seemed to bond in. We called the game, "I Love You But I Just Can't Smile," which is what you said as your opponent did whatever they could to make you smile. Normally quick to smile, our son had an iron will. He could and did resist smiling. His mother could almost always win the game by getting him to smile.

Remembering His Smile

I miss that smile.
One of the first times
I remember it was when
He was 18 months old.
I had told him, "No!"
As he was trying to peel
The cover off an electrical outlet.

He smiled big,
"It's okay, Dad.
Let me do what I want."
Then he turned back to
Work on the outlet cover.

He was a happy baby.
As he aged, he smiled less
Continuing to work us
Every way he could.

Strong willed,
Defiant, rebellious
Oppositional
Are all adjectives that
Described him well,
Always turning toward
The dangerous and forbidden.
Electrical sockets were

Just the first inkling.

He had a great smile.
An impish grin.
A charming laugh.
Sometimes it was a cover
For insecurities
And uncertainties.
But mostly
Smiling came from
His heart.

As years wore on
He smiled less.
Becoming the serious philosopher
Who struggled to find meaning,
The Socratic questioner,
Who confronted his own
Doubts and delighted
In uncovering yours.

But his smile would return
From time to time.
He would blow a kiss
To the biggest and baddest
Rough motorcycle rider
Just to throw him off.
Then he would smile.

He brought a surprising
Joy to those around him.
Who continue to miss
His smile
As I do.

I treasure the photographs, the videos, the websites, the social media pages—anything that helps me remember even though the memories bring tears. I love to talk about my son to those who knew him. I love to share stories and review memories. It is painful, but it is a way of staying connected to him. I am learning to ignore those who criticize me for focusing on the past. This is how I deal with my grief, trying to hang on to my son. Our relationships with the people we love, even the ones who are gone, bring the greatest value to our lives. I hold on to all I can.

Encouragement

In your grieving feel free to do whatever you need to do in order to remember your love one. Keep his room exactly the same if that helps. Don't give away her clothes until you are ready. Adopt his dog. Transfer her car title to you. Treasure his ashes. Use her purse. Remembering is so important. Sometimes it helps to hold on to something tangible.

Moving Forward

1. Reflect on you favorite memories. Write them down or record them.

2. Make a "memory chest" with items that belonged to them or that remind you of them.

3. Display photos or other items in a prominent place that bring memories of good times.

4. Make a scrapbook with photos, stories, announcements, anything that helps hold on to memories.

5. Participate in Holy Communion/Eucharist/Lord's Supper as a healing sacrament.

6. Read and reflect on the tangible way Jesus gave us to remember his death--1 Corinthians 11:23-25.

Prayer

Lord, when we observe Holy Communion, we remember your sacrifice for us so that a new covenant might be established with you. Bread and wine are tangible reminders of your death for us, Lord Jesus. On the night you established this sacred meal, you also gave us a new command to love one another. Now that we have lost one whom we have loved, we pray for you to comfort us as we remember. Although remembering is painful for us, we ask that you would help us honor and remember the one we have lost. Even though our remembering may keep us from smiling and being happy, we pray you would fill us with the hope that we will see our loved one again, just as you promised your friends around that table. Give us hope in our painful memories that we will embrace again. Amen.

20 Losing Him Again

But of others there is no memory;
they have perished as though they had never existed;
they have become as though they had never been born,
they and their children after them.
Sirach 44:9

In conversations with people who have suffered loss, one of the fears they have expressed to me is that of forgetting their loved one. A widow once told me, "I am forgetting what he looked like. So I often look at photos of him. I am also forgetting what he sounded like. I keep trying to remember."

We think we'll never forget the one who was so important to us. And we probably will not unless afflicted with Alzheimer's or other form of dementia. But the memories fade. Memory tends to be "re-creations" of different bits and pieces in our minds. Most of us don't remember events like video recordings. After time memories change and fade and have to be reconstructed, and are often wrongly remembered. Just ask an attorney how unreliable eyewitnesses are. We are not reliable because our memories are not.

So what does that mean for our losses. It means the longer we are in grief, the less accurately we remember our loved ones. That would be natural. But the fog of grief clouds those memories even more. So it is like a second loss, losing them again. It is scary and depressing that we cannot remember like we want. I want to replay every scene of every day of my son's life. So few stand out in my memory. Often my wife and I do not remember the same event the same way.

Losing My Grip

We lost our son in an instant
On May 20, 2013 about 9:30 AM
Or was it 10:00?
near Lancaster, California
Killed when he crashed his motorcycle into a mountain
On the _____ Highway
On a road he traveled daily
After riding 200,000 miles on motorcycles in Los Angeles
Over five years as a motorcycle courier
Working for _____.

The rope is beginning to slip
Through my hands.

Born on July 21, 1980 at _____ Hospital
In Louisville, KY.
He had some mysterious rash and fever
The physicians checked him for everything
Including spinal meningitis
It was a scary time. He remained in the hospital for
Ten days or was it two weeks?

The strands ratchet slowly
Through my clenched fist.

He was a happy baby.
His first word was "popcorn"
Or was it "Daddy"?

He was about 10 ½ months old
When he learned to walk.
Actually he ran.

104

He never stopped.

The strands move faster as
I try to hold on to each one.

He played football
Was the biggest kid
On the team
Was it the Saints
Or the Giants?

He loved animals.
He was good with them.
He worked on a horse
Farm in Tallahassee
Was it 1999 or 2000?

He was good with his hands.
He worked as a carpenter
In Colorado
What city was that?

He moved to Sacramento
To work in a cabinet
Shop with Matt
In _____.

The rope is burning my hands.

Lord, help me remember the good
And the bad.
It all seems to be fading
How he looked
How he sounded
What he liked
Am I losing him again?
Losing him forever?

Help me to hold on to him.

Help me remember.
Help me grip
The rope.

My memory is not what I would want when it comes to my son. I want to remember everything about him. Yet I cannot. It adds to my sadness that I cannot bring to mind all the scenes from the past, which makes photos of him all the more important. This is another part of my grief experience, which I share with others.

Encouragement

Mourning has many facets to it. You may experience difficulty remembering your loved one. This is normal, not only because of the fog of grief, but because for most of us our memories are actually re-creations of past reality. We take different pieces and join them into a picture that makes sense to us. Some of the pieces of the puzzle are missing so our brain fills in. It may not be so important that you remember exactly what happened. Sometimes remembering the emotions that you experienced as you reflect on the past, can help replay scenes in your mind.

Moving Forward

1. Make a new photo album of your loved one, either physical or virtual, or both.

2. Write down your favorite scenes as you remember them.

3. Talk with someone who shared special days, like birthdays, family outings, vacations--about happy times you experienced with your loved one.

4. Play their favorite songs.

5. Read and reflect on 2 Timothy 1:3-5.

Prayer

God you remember us and all who have lived. You remember the one we lost. Help us to bring to mind those scenes from the past, those happy moments and joyful occasions, which may help heal our pain of grief. When we can't remember, fill us with your grace. Amen.

106

WHY GOD?

21 Did God Blink?

I lift up my eyes to the hills —
from where will my help come?
My help comes from the LORD,
who made heaven and earth.
He will not let your foot be moved;
he who keeps you will not slumber.
He who keeps Israel
will neither slumber nor sleep.
The LORD is your keeper;
the LORD is your shade at your right hand.
The sun shall not strike you by day,
nor the moon by night.
The LORD will keep you from all evil;
he will keep your life.
The LORD will keep
your going out and your coming in
from this time on and forevermore.
Psalm 121

The Bible affirms that the Lord does not sleep but always watches over us, always takes care of us. But what happened when my son crashed? Wasn't God watching over him? How do we understand

107

the role of a loving and all-powerful God when the worst happens?

On Monday morning May 20, 2013, Yvonne and I prayed for God to watch over our son Samuel as we often did. But later that morning as he was riding his motorcycle from Lancaster to Los Angeles on the Angeles Forest Highway, a road he loved to ride, he crashed. Why didn't God protect him? Why didn't he walk away this time? Why didn't he get back up on a scratched-up bike and ride on into work as he had done before? Why wasn't God watching over him? Did God blink?

Why God?

The throbbing query
Of a parent's shattered heart
Why didn't you do something to stop it?
Why didn't you do something?!

All powerful, all wise
All loving
They don't jive
These praises we offer
To One who could have
But did not.

Am I ungrateful?
I thanked you many times
For watching over him
Flying an inch away from sudden death.
You were there
Keeping him safe
Time and time again.

Had he so offended you
Or had I
That you turned your back
Letting him die?

"My God, My God

Why have you forsaken me?"
Was your Son's cry
As he died upon that tree.

But my son was
No celestial celebrity
So why should I expect your
Continued protection detail?
Why shouldn't I expect
A bloody end?

After all he rode a motorcycle
Which is reason enough
For many to say
He deserved to die,
Such a dangerous way
To fly.

Do you so easily
Discard a life,
Like the rubber glove
Tossed by an EMT?

Covered in dried blood
I found it three weeks
Later in the rocks
Dislodged from the impact
Of his body and his bike
Against that mountain.

Evidence that
At least someone
Had tried
To save him.

Where were you, Lord?
Why had you gone?
Too late now
Never mind.

True you showed up
Three days later
For your Son
"All part of a plan"
Is what believers say.

But those of us whose hearts
Have died with those we love
Are buried
In the darkness of the tomb
Waiting
Wondering
Why?

There is no end to the questions. For me I have found no answers that truly satisfy my longing to know why. I have read the popular books about why bad things happen. I have read the scholarly books as well. No one can square a God who is omnipotent and all-loving with the tragedies that occur. None of the answers satisfy. They all fall short philosophically and theologically. Would having an answer ease my pain anyway?

The easy answers people give are offensive to me: "It was God's will." So you are accusing God of killing my son. "Everything happens for a reason." But you cannot give the reason. If God is super intelligent, could He not have come up with a better ending for my son's life. I can certainly come up with a better one and I'm not as smart as God.

"He's in a better place." How do you know that? Did God reveal his judgment about my son's case to you? You may believe everyone is in a better place after death, but dumping your doctrine on me does not explain why this happened to my son. I've learned to listen politely.

I'm learning the most honest thing for me is to live with the questions and continue believing in a good and gracious God. In other words, I'm learning to live with the personal pain of this paradox. It has taken months to begin to get there.

Encouragement

If you find an answer that makes sense to you, then latch on to it. Each of us is different. There may be a truth that helps you get through this. Wonderful!

If you cannot make sense of the situation, that's okay. The greatest minds on the planet have not been able to explain with any satisfaction why evil happens in a world created and managed by a good God. Although the questions can be tortuous, honestly admitting we don't know can be helpful. Yes, you will have to endure people who think they have all the answers, and worse yet, who want to persuade you to agree with them. They apparently assume that if you buy into their answer, you will feel better. Avoid them. Do not harm them, but avoid them.

Moving Forward

1. Read Psalm 22. Can you relate to the sense of abandonment and despair that the psalmist feels? Do you share his continued trust in God?

2. Join a grief support group where others have similar emotions and questions.

Prayer

God of the universe, we admit we do not understand. We get angry when we think of how you did not step in to protect, to heal, to rescue . . . . Help us to be comforted by your presence even as we feel you have forsaken us. May we know your grace and mercy in the midst of our personal confusion and our human lack of understanding. Amen.

22 Time and Chance

Again I saw that under the sun the race is not to the swift, nor the battle to the strong, nor bread to the wise, nor riches to the intelligent, nor favor to the skillful; but time and chance happen to them all. For no one can anticipate the time of disaster. Like fish taken in a cruel net, and like birds caught in a snare, so mortals are snared at a time of calamity, when it suddenly falls upon them.
Ecclesiastes 9:11-12

Six months ago today, our son Samuel was killed in a motorcycle accident. Yvonne and I had prayed that morning for God to watch over him, as we had prayed many times. Previously I had even commented that my son being a motorcycle courier had improved my prayer life. At his house when we celebrated his life with his motorcycle courier friends, an older one, probably my age, said, "With what we do it's not a matter of 'if' but 'when' we all end up like Sam." Was it inevitable that if you ride a motorcycle 200,000 miles through the traffic of Los Angeles that you would eventually lose the odds? Are there odds? Is God in control of everything that happens?

Who's in Charge?

Some of my pious friends
Both Christian and Muslim

Point to you,
O God,
As the One who
Is in charge.

They are too polite
To say
They believe
You killed my son,
You caused
Him to crash.

Was it judgment
For sin?
His or mine
That you took him
In his prime?

Was his
Number up?
What was the reason
That everything happened
That day on
That mountain curve
In that moment?

These friends paint
You red of tooth
And claw
Killing off creatures
Great and small.

Your apparent
Atrocities and myriad
Injustices will
All be worked
Out in the sweet
Bye and bye.

And if not you,
Then who is
In control?

Must there be
Someone to blame
For cancer that kills
A Three-year-old,
Tsunamis that wipe
Out entire villages,
Tornadoes that
Tear apart towns?

We, who believe
In a power greater
Than ourselves,
Must come to grips
With how we think
You wield
Your scepter,
O King eternal.

Are we to learn
Like ancient Job
That you take extended
Vacations?
Or that you allow your son Satan
To torment the faithful?
Did he go too far with
My son?

My tiny mind tries
To decipher
The universe
And its Creator.

If you are not in charge
Why pray?
Why ask for favors

From an absentee
Landlord?

Are you the clockmaker,
Who made it,
Wound it up,
Then moved on
To other worlds?

Was it all determined
With the flick
Of your finger
On the first domino?

I prefer the
Crucified God
Who knows
My grief,
Who cries out,
"My God, my God,
Why have you forsaken me!?"

You are
My Light
My only hope
Inside this tomb
Of death and darkness
Where my questions
Echo back to me.

I prefer to think like the writer of Ecclesiastes that there are accidents. "Time and chance" happen to everyone. There is randomness to the universe that God created. God does not cause every event that happens. If we believe that God causes everything, then God appears to be more evil than our worst imagination. Then God caused dictators like Hitler and Idi Amin to torture and kill millions of people. Then the Lord caused the rape of infants and toddlers. The atrocities of war and the ravages of disease must be ascribed to God along with tornadoes that wipe out towns and earthquakes that destroy cities. Then how can we conceive of God as good?

I believe that God is aware of everything that happens and that God is with us in every circumstance. God was with my son in that instant he crashed into the side of that mountain as God had always been with him, even if my son did not always acknowledge God. God was with my wife, daughter and me when we got the bad news. Jesus said that when a sparrow falls to the ground, God is there. Jesus said, "Are not two little birds sold for a penny? Yet not one of them will fall to the ground without your Father (being there)." (Matthew 10:29, author's translation). I see God as fundamentally benevolent, as goodness, not evil. I see God as the One who suffers with us, not the one making us suffer.

Encouragement

You have questions, questions for which there are no satisfactory answers. Brilliant minds have tried to answer the question of how we understand a good God in a world where evil happens. They have failed. Scholarly books I have read on this subject say 1) God chooses not to be in control of everything and/or 2) all the unjust cruelties of this life will be rectified in heaven. Neither answer satisfies my mind nor soothes my heart. If they help you, I am glad. Even though we wonder why God did not answer our prayers for healing, for protection, for well-being, we do not find satisfactory answers. People say, "There are no unanswered prayers. God sometimes says, 'No.'" But that does nothing to answer our questions of why a good God did not intervene to do good for our loved one. Wrestling with this question may be part of your grief, as it is part of mine.

Moving Forward

1. Read and reflect on Ecclesiastes 9:1-12.

2. Participate in a Bible Study or small group where you have the opportunity to discuss your questions.

Prayer

God, we have prayed, but you have not answered our prayers. We do not understand why. May we sense your presence with us. May you grant us that peace that goes beyond understanding. Amen.

23 If Only. . .

"If I sin, what do I do to you, you watcher of humanity?
Why have you made me your target?
Why have I become a burden to you?
Why do you not pardon my transgression
and take away my iniquity?
For now I shall lie in the earth;
you will seek me, but I shall not be."
Job 7:20-21

Job was suffering terribly. When we suffer we want answers. We want an explanation. When we experience loss, we question everything. In our attempt to understand why our loved one died, we question God and ourselves. Such questions are not necessarily productive in terms of finding answers. But they are normal.

"If"

If I had been different,
A more protective dad
My son would not
Have died.

If I had done

117

Things differently
He would still
Be alive.

If I had not taught him
To ride and to love
Riding motorcycles

. . . .

If California
Had not made the white line
Between the lanes
A legal lane for motorcycles

. . . .

If legal firms did not
Use motorcycle
Riders as couriers
To fly between cars
And beat deadlines

. . . .

If he had not bought
A house he could afford
An hour and a half
Away from his job
In downtown LA

. . . .

If he had not been so excited about
Our visit to see him
To take him to see
The Grand Canyon
And Yosemite
He would have not overslept and
Been rushing to work

. . . .

If there weren't lose rocks

118

On the shoulder of the road

. . .

If he had found a safer job

. . . .

If he had gone back to school

. . .

If he had kept working with Matt

. . . .

If the driver of the muscle car
Had not

. . .

If . . .

The questions tumble over and over in our minds. Like a lopsided dryer, which will not stop scraping while tossing the clothes again and again and again. "Why did he die? What could I have done differently? Why did I . . . ? If only . . . then he or she would not have died." We try to re-make the past so that our loved one does not die. Our questioning makes no logical sense but is driven by our grief. Even months later, our minds can go back into this cross-examination of ourselves.

So many times I have questioned why I taught my son to ride a motorcycle. At the time he was looking for cheap transportation. Had I known that is how he would die twelve years later, I would have refused. But what if he had been killed in an automobile accident? Should I have not taught him how to drive a car? Such self-recrimination is pointless. The emotions that overwhelm us can devastate our sense of self-worth. Even though I still occasionally find myself asking "if only," I know that I cannot change what happened. I must learn to live with what I have done, what he did and what others did to contribute to my son's death. Finally I am learning to let go of the guilt and the questions—most days.

119

Encouragement

No, you are not going crazy if you continue to ask questions about what you could have done for things to be different. Guilt drives those self-interrogations in our minds. It's normal, but certainly difficult. Blaming yourself is a normal part of grief even if it makes no sense logically. As much as you can, absolve yourself, forgive yourself and stop beating yourself up. As you are able begin to let go of the "if only's".

Moving Forward

1. Talk with a counselor or trusted friend about how you feel. Share your thoughts, questions and feelings with them.

2. Pray to God to help you turn off the questions that continue to torture your mind.

3. Read and reflect on Job 3, particularly Job's questions in verses 11-26.

Prayer

Lord, we are guilty of many things. We often fail you and others. We confess to you our failure to love you and one another in the way you have taught us. Forgive us for our mistakes. Set us free from the guilt that enslaves our minds and hearts. Amen.

24 "Everything Happens for a Reason?"

"As for me, is my complaint addressed to mortals?
Why should I not be impatient?
Look at me, and be appalled,
and lay your hand upon your mouth.
When I think of it I am dismayed,
and shuddering seizes my flesh.
Why do the wicked live on,
reach old age, and grow mighty in power?
Their children are established in their presence,
and their offspring before their eyes.
Their houses are safe from fear,
and no rod of God is upon them."
Job 21:4-9

The Book of Job in the Bible is one of the greatest pieces of literature in the world. The protagonist Job wrestles with why he has lost all his possessions and why all his children have been killed and why he has been afflicted with a terrible disease. Until disaster struck him, he had understood God causes good things to happen to righteous people and bad to befall the wicked. His friends still think that way. The disasters, which have crushed this "perfect" or "blameless," man, as the Bible calls him, contradict the idea of a just God in a moral universe. Now he feels the rod of God upon his back when he has done nothing to deserve it. At the same time he points to the prosperity of the wicked, who reject God and afflict their fellow humans.

My Reasonable God

Tell me, O God
What reason
Can you give
For the death
Of my son?

Speak to me
I beg like ancient Job
For an answer
To why?

If you are behind this,
Give me your rationale
Not only for me
But for all who grieve
Undeserved pain.

"It was his time."
"It was meant to be."
"Everything happens
For a reason."

My friends try to encourage
Me with the thought that
You are in control
Of all details.
Are you?

Does your master plan
Include young men crashing,
Cancers for babies,
Mothers dying in childbirth,
Tortures and murders?

Do you inspire the perpetrators
To devastate other's lives?
Do you micromanage this world
As we know it?

Jesus said you
Number our hairs.
Do you also tear them out
In the grip of a rapist?

Do you make them
Fall out with chemotherapy
From the cancer you inflicted?

Do you shave women's heads
In pogroms?

They make you out
To be a monster with
A diabolical plan
That includes
Atrocities for which I
Would be incarcerated
Or worse.

They attribute a rationality
To actions that are unreasonable
Making you the subject of
Criminal cruelties.

Like Job's friends
They claim you are just
In punishing all who do evil.

The afflicted
In utero,
In the neonatal unit
In the memory wing
In the prison camp

123

Are getting what they
Deserve.

Their testimony to your
Power and control
Comes at the cost
Of your love and grace.

I choose the latter
Longing for your
Presence
To lift my broken spirit
To calm my
Questioning mind.

I have never been a determinist or a Calvinist because I cannot believe God causes people to sin and then punishes them for it. Nor can I believe that God causes all the suffering in the world as part of his divine plan. That makes God out to be an evil monster. It's not the image of God I gain from reading about Jesus Christ in the Gospels. I am left without answers as to why, like Job. God said that Job's friends, who had defended God's integrity and thrown doubt on Job's, were wrong. Job had constantly accused God of injustice and complained about God's mistreatment of him. In the end God agreed with Job (Job 42:7-8). That is an incredible admission on God's part, or is it?

Encouragement
You may not be able to answer why your loved one was taken. You may struggle with why a good and loving God, who is all-powerful, could have allowed such a thing to happen. I wish I could give you an answer that is not the same "pat answers" Job's friends gave, which turned out to be wrong. You may have to learn to live with uncertainty and gnawing questions. I have come to understand this as a painful part of the grief process.

Moving Forward
1. Read and reflect on Job 21.

2. Write down all the reasons you think your loss was unfair.

3. Write down reasons you are grateful to God for your loved one's life.

Prayer

God, we do not understand. We know that you are good, fair, just, loving, all-powerful, all-knowing . . . . We cannot grasp why you did not intervene to heal, protect, guard, guide and preserve our loved one. Help us in our lack of understanding to live with this uncertainty in the midst of our grief. We give you thanks. Amen.

25 "Lord, If Only You Had Been Here!"

When Mary came where Jesus was and saw him, she knelt at his feet and said to him, "Lord, if you had been here, my brother would not have died." When Jesus saw her weeping, and the Jews who came with her also weeping, he was greatly disturbed in spirit and deeply moved. He said, "Where have you laid him?" They said to him, "Lord, come and see." Jesus began to weep. So the Jews said, "See how he loved him!" But some of them said, "Could not he who opened the eyes of the blind man have kept this man from dying?
John 11:32-37

Mary's sister Martha had said the same thing to Jesus, "Lord, if you had been here, my brother would not have died" (John 11:21). Apparently they had seen Jesus perform miracles and had confidence that Jesus would have healed their brother and his friend Lazarus. Of course, the complaint of both sisters reveals a faith on their part. Their chastisement of Jesus also reveals their anger and confusion at his absence. Then Jesus raises their brother Lazarus from the dead.

Part of the message of the passage is that even though it appears that the Lord is absent, he will come through in the end. In fact, in the story Jesus has delayed coming on purpose in order for the sick Lazarus to die so that Jesus could bring him back to life. The point of the story in the raising of Lazarus is that Jesus is even more powerful than death.

The story also teaches us something about God's absence. As we wail and lament over God not being there to heal our loved one or to protect them, the story points to a reality beyond this life, beyond protection or healing. Although Jesus raised Lazarus from the dead, Lazarus would die again. His sisters would once more mourn his passing. But that would come after Jesus' own death and resurrection, which changes everything. Lazarus being raised from the dead is a preview of what will happen with Jesus Christ.

Those of us who have experienced loss live in the state of "Lord if you had been here . . . ." Yet Jesus' life, death and resurrection point to a reality beyond this life. We see a glimpse of it in this story in John's Gospel. In grief we think we live in the absence of God. This story reminds us God is never absent and his power to bring life even in death calls us to walk in that life-giving presence.

Why Didn't He Come?

I struggle to move.
I cannot make my muscles act.
Paralyzed, I long for light
Long for the dawn
But it does not come.
This oppressive night crushes
My soul.

I am awake
But cannot breathe.
I am conscious
But cannot shout for help.

They think I died.
So they wrapped me up,
Put me in this cave
To rot.

"Lazarus, Come out!"

127

So this is how it ends.
Everyone thinking I am gone.
Yet I heard all that they said,
Listened as my sisters cried,
Wishing I could tell them,
No, I am not dead. I am alive!

Am I?
Do the dead know what we do to them?
Why does my spirit
Refuse to leave
This carcass?

Why can't I abandon this
Bound up body,
This decaying corpse?

"Lazarus, Come out!"

Where was my friend Jesus?
Why didn't he come?
Could he have healed me?
Didn't he even care?

Was he so busy he could not
Bother to come to the aid
Of a friend?
Why leave me to suffer
And die?

I feel no more pain.
Except the anguish
Of being abandoned
By the one I thought
Would never let me down.

"Lazarus, Come out!"

The disease has done its damage.

The insects have begun
To work on what is left
Of what was me.

My God, My God
Why have you forsaken me?!
All I know is your absence,
Total darkness.

They prayed for Jesus
To come, but he did not,
For God to be merciful
But He was not.

"Lazarus, Come out!"

God is always ready to comfort us. But we are not always ready to be comforted. God brings light and life, but sometimes we prefer the dark. God does not stop calling us even when we do not hear. I eventually did begin to sense God's comforting presence but only after months and months of mourning.

Encouragement
As soon as you are able, allow God to love you, to comfort you, to take care of you. You may experience that comfort through friends and family, through time in prayer or in many different ways. Be as open as you can to receive the light that God wants to shine in your darkness.

Moving Forward
1. Share with a friend or counselor your frustration at God's not having stepped in to help, to heal or to protect.

2. Write a letter to God expressing your disappointment that God did not intervene according to what you wanted.

3. Read and reflect on John 11 and the hope of resurrection.

Prayer
Lord, when we feel like you don't care, help us to learn the depth of your love. When we think there is no hope or no reason to go on, carry us through those difficult times. Thank you for never forsaking us even when we are convinced you have abandoned us.

INJUSTICE, MURDER, AND SUICIDE

26 They Had It Coming

*As Jesus walked along, he saw a man blind from birth. His disciples
asked him, "Rabbi, who sinned, this man or his parents, that he was born
blind?" Jesus answered, "Neither this man nor his parents sinned; he
was born blind so that God's works might be revealed in him."*
John 9:1-3

Then Jesus healed the blind man. Jesus' disciples had an easy
explanation for why a person would suffer. It was a popular
explanation. Anyone, who suffers or experiences misfortune,
deserves it. Such thinking is still prevalent today.

"They Had It Coming"

My friend was diagnosed
With lung cancer.
First question they ask,
"Did he smoke?"

So what if he did?
(He did not.)
Does it give you comfort
To offer an explanation of

131

Why he is sick?

Killed in a motorcycle crash.
"Motorcycles
Are dangerous.
I would never ride a motorcycle."

Heart attack.
"Was she overweight?
Didn't exercise, did she?"

Killed in an auto accident.
"Were they wearing their seat belts?
Were they driving a small car?
Were they speeding?"

Committed suicide.
"Must have been depressed."

Simplistic analysis
Cannot begin to unravel
What happened.

Aren't the events
Of our lives
Interwoven with
Myriad causes for
Every effect and
Thousands of effects
From a single cause?

Do you assume
You are safe?
Does your brain tell
You that if you avoid
Obvious risks
That you are going to be okay
Because you are a good person?

132

"Bad things only happen to bad people.
People get what they deserve."

A parrot squawks
In a cage in the zoo
Telling all the other
Animals why they suffer.

He only speaks
What he has heard
With no understanding
Of his own words.

My son died in a motorcycle crash. I had taught him how to ride a motorcycle in the parking lot of the church I had served in Tallahassee. I helped him get his first Honda Rebel 250. On the morning he crashed he was riding a Honda NC 700 into Los Angeles where he worked as a motorcycle courier.

We were sitting in an attorney's office sorting out our son's affairs a few weeks after his death. She expressed her condolences. When we explained how our son died, the attorney said, "I never allowed either of my boys to ride a motorcycle." I heard her say, "People who ride motorcycles get killed on them. It's your fault for allowing him to ride a motorcycle in the first place. You are to blame for his death." Others volunteered that they were responsible parents and never let their children near a motorcycle. Who sinned, this man or his parents? I heard, "His father."

Two parishioners, who were interested in having a child baptized, were in my office. In the course of the conversation they asked if I had children. I spoke of my daughter and shared about my son's death in a motorcycle accident. The wife (a highly educated person) responded out of the blue, "Motorcycle riders are _____ (expletive)." Her husband tried to cover up her judgmental vulgar statement to a grieving father. I sat in disbelief.

When someone suffers, we to want a simple answer for why it happened. The disciples of Jesus thought, as did most Jews of their day, that all suffering was punishment for sin. Jesus did not buy it. Neither do I. Bad things happen to good people every day. Tragedies strike. There are no pat answers that make sense and certainly none that help people who grieve. I learned that sometimes people say really stupid things with no thought how their words will impact others or what the implication of their shallow explanations mean.

Encouragement

I encourage you to ignore people who imply that somehow you deserved this loss. Stay away from those who blame the victim. Remember that Jesus did not blame those who suffered, but helped them instead. Fill your life with people who want to help and heal. Avoid those who put you down, especially in this time of grief. You don't have to put up with that and you certainly don't need it.

Questions for Reflection

1. Why do people give pat answers to tragedy?

2. Do you get angry when someone offers a simplistic answer to explain your loss?

3. How do you respond to someone else's loss?

4. Read and reflect on John 9.

Prayer

God keep us from pretending that we know why things happen. Only you know why. Help us not to be judgmental of others, especially in their loss. Instead of putting others down, fill us with compassion. As we grieve, give us the courage to stand up to those who blame victims and the wisdom to stay away from those who judge us and others. Surround us with people like Jesus so that we may find healing. Amen.

27 No Justice

Even when I cry out, 'Violence!' I am not answered;
I call aloud, but there is no justice.
Job 19:7

O daughter Babylon, you devastator!
Happy shall they be who pay you back
what you have done to us!
Happy shall they be who take your little ones
and dash them against the rock!
Psalm 137:8-9

Job longs for justice. The psalmist longs for revenge, for someone to kill Babylonian babies, as the Babylonians had killed Israelite babies. Revenge? Justice?

It's been a year since her daughter was murdered. I meet her in the hallway and ask how she is doing and how the investigation is going. She says the authorities give little hope of ever finding out who took her daughter's life. She says there will never be justice for her daughter. Too many times families of those who are killed find there is no justice for their loved ones. Some cases make it to trial, but there is not always justice there as the parents of Trayvon Martin experienced. George Zimmerman killed their son Trayvon Martin on February 26, 2012, but was found not guilty. Sometimes there is no evidence that a crime was committed (even if one was)

135

or there is not sufficient evidence to bring the guilty person to justice.

No Justice for My Son

Call the witnesses.
Let them testify
Though they will never
Go to court.
Let the sun admit
To shining brightly
And the pavement
To being dry
That morning.

Cross examine the
Mountain that
Bore the impact
Of body and bike.

Let the road testify
That my son had ridden
Him every morning
On his way to work.

Let the Honda NC700
Motorcycle enter its
Complaint of
Being clipped by
The muscle car
Which caused it to go down.

Let the motorcycle
Point to the broken piece
Bruised by the bumper
Of the car.

Make the Challenger
Tell the truth

That his damaged wheel
Was not the result
Of dislodged rocks
But contact with the
Two-wheeler.

His friends have
Gone on record.
My son was
Too skilled,
Too experienced
To crash on
His daily route on
Angeles Forest Highway

Let the record show for
Five and a half years,
200,000 miles on the streets
And roads of Los Angeles
Proved him to be
The most talented
Rider of all
Motorcycle couriers
In Southern California.

The driver of the car
Will never have to plead
Guilt or innocence.

The highway patrol
Bought
His story.

No evidence
Was needed for them
To reach a verdict.

No appeal would be heard
Because the voice

Of my son
Was silenced.

The rocks around
By the road
On the canyon curve
Continue to
Cry out for justice.

Am I the only one
Who can hear them?

In my anger
I wince every time
I see that model
Muscle car.

As a father
I was unable to protect him
And now
Unwilling to seek revenge,
Unable to get justice
For him.

I cry out to God
With the ancient psalmist,
"Let it be done to him
What he did to my son!"
But nothing happens.

A Word from the "Defendant"

"I told them I was
On the way to
A funeral.
That my riders
Were ill.
That's why I was going
So slow.

138

I was not at fault.
He should not have
Tried to pass me
On a double yellow line.
He deserved what he got.
He was going too fast.

Surely there was no
Mark on his shattered
Motorcycle
That can prove
That my car clipped him.

Nobody saw it.
He is dead.
They cannot prove
I did anything wrong.

Got my wheel replaced
They will never know.

Their attorney called.
He knows I did something
To cause that young man
To crash.

Will they sue me?
Will I lose what little I have?
Will they take my muscle car?

I only jerked
The steering wheel
A little to the left.
I didn't intend to kill him.

I just wanted
To scare him
To slow him down.

I didn't want him to pass me.

I shouldn't go to prison
For a little jerk of the wheel.
He was the one breaking the law,
Not me.

Those motorcycle riders are
All #^*$%! anyway,
Always passing
Always cutting in.
Sooner or later
They crash.
Everybody knows that.
Don't blame me!"

I'm learning what it's like to not get justice, to be powerless to do anything to right a wrong that apparently led to my son's death. I've gotten that stare from authorities, which says, "I'm not going to do anything about this." History, large and small, is always written by the survivors. The dead do not get a chance to tell their side. My son was forever silenced. I have to let go of a desire for revenge, and a longing for justice. This is a part of my grief I am coming to accept.

Encouragement

If another person was responsible for your loved one's death, you may wish harm on the person or persons responsible. This is normal and natural. You know and keep telling yourself that even if you could take revenge on them, it would not bring back the one you lost. Even if they are convicted and spend the rest of their lives in prison, it may not bring you the peace you want. Medical malpractice, homicide, vehicular manslaughter, friendly fire, negligence on the part of caretakers and other human causes of death are often left unresolved. This adds to the "normal" grief of losing someone you love. It is also an aspect of your suffering that has to be accepted for what it is: injustice. Sometimes ones we love are the victims. So we become victims. Knowing this does not make it any easier. But the only path that can lead to healing is ultimately accepting what has happened, and by the grace of God eventually learning to forgive.

Moving Forward

1. On your way to acceptance you may want to write down what you would like to see happen to the perpetrator in your loved one's case. Make the punishment as severe as you want (like the psalmist above). You may want to destroy this after you have written it down.

2. Talk to someone you trust about how much you want justice and how frustrated and angry you are.

3. Read Psalm 137. How do your relate to this horrific idea of getting revenge?

Prayer

God, we are human. We want revenge. We want justice. We pray that you will help us accept that we cannot take revenge without committing a crime against them and a sin against you. In our anger we pray for self-control. In our sadness, we pray for comfort. We pray for justice for our loved ones. If that is not possible in this life, help us to learn to live with injustice. We pray that with time and grace you will grant us mercy and help us to come to the point of praying for mercy for those who have hurt our loved ones. Amen.

28 One Was Taken

You turn us back to dust,
and say, "Turn back, you mortals."
For a thousand years in your sight
are like yesterday when it is past,
or like a watch in the night.
You sweep them away; they are like a dream,
like grass that is renewed in the morning;
in the morning it flourishes and is renewed;
in the evening it fades and withers.
Psalm 90:3-6

Our daughter was born six weeks early with birth defects. She was immediately transferred to Riley Hospital for Children in Indianapolis, where she underwent surgery. At first she was in an incubator in ICU. Then for weeks she was in a unit with babies in rows of clear plastic bassinettes. Most were hooked up to IVs. Across the aisle from our little Rebekah Joy was Abigail. Compared to our premature Rebekah who was struggling to get to four pounds, Abigail at six months, was triple her size. Abigail had a heart defect. Her parents were faithful to be there every day with their daughter as we were. One day Abigail was not there. I asked the nurse where she was. She said, "Abigail did not make it." We were shocked and saddened.

In the lobby of the hospital I would take breaks with our active three-year-old son. One day as he explored the huge glass-enclosed area, a woman came to the same window with her two-year-old in tow. He was sitting quietly in a red wagon, too weak to play like my son. He was hooked up to an IV with chemicals to combat his leukemia. His mother and I talked a little. With a heavy sadness she told me about his condition. I felt guilt that my son was so big and healthy while this little boy was emaciated.

After six weeks of hospitalization, we were able to bring our daughter Rebekah Joy home on Christmas Eve. We were elated. It was the best Christmas present we could have hoped for. While we were rejoicing, Abigail's parents would have a deeply sad Christmas.

Why is one spared and another not? There is a passage in the Bible that has always raised this issue for me. In Acts, chapter 12, James, one of Jesus' inner circle (Peter, James and John) was arrested. Herod Agrippa had James executed. The city reacted in a positive way so Herod arrested Peter and planned to execute him. Then Peter was miraculously set free from prison. Why was James not also spared? Why didn't the miracle happen to James? Why was Abigail taken and not our daughter? Why did my son die and not I? Loss blinds us with the glaring spotlight of the unfairness of life and death.

Numbered Lives

Is it all random?
Is there rhyme or reason
To life and death?
Does your number
Come up
Like in the lottery?

When the bullets
Whiz by your ears
But take out your buddy
Is it luck or fate?

Why should one live

143

Only a few days
While another lives
Beyond a hundred years?

Babies, who never
Had a chance.
Others squander
The life they
Are given.

So many broken
Threads in this
Tapestry, you are weaving,
O Lord.

The prayer of Moses
Blames your anger
Over our iniquities
For your command
"Turn back to dust!"

But what sin has a
Baby committed?
Yet powerful perpetrators
Of oppression and injustice
Live on and on, unrestrained.

Are we no more than
Rain lilies in the desert
Sprouting only for a day
When a rare shower comes?

Yet you go on and on
A thousand years
Like a watch in the night
For you.

How can I who am ephemeral
Question the eternal?

Could I understand
Your response?

So Moses teaches us
To number our days
That we may gain wisdom.

Will wisdom
Give answers
Or teach
Silence?

Will we learn
How to think
Or how
To be
When others
Are not.

In my mourning the loss of my son, I have felt guilt that I remain. Parents should die before their children. Survivor's guilt, as some call it, grows out of a sense that it's not fair. Will I ever understand why he was taken and I survive? Why did Abigail die and Rebekah thrive? Why was James martyred so soon but Peter continued many years before he faced the same fate? The unfairness of it all frustrates my mind. Can I learn to live with questions I cannot answer? It's a part of my grief that I cannot make sense of it all.

Encouragement
"It's not fair." That phrase keeps slapping you in the face. You may feel guilty that you survived when your loved one did not. You may be frustrated trying to understand why you lost your loved one. The questions may keep piling on smothering your mind. Having to come to grips with not comprehending why they died and you survived, is painful. When someone offers you pat answers, know that better minds have tried and failed to comprehend the mysteries of life and death. In the end you have to figure out how to go on with the overwhelming sense of the

unfairness of your loss. Perhaps answers will come when we leave this temporal world and become part of the eternal. Then it may not matter at all when God becomes "our dwelling place."

Moving Forward
1. Read and reflect on the story of James' execution and Peter's miraculous escape in Acts 12:1-18.

2. Write a list of reasons why your loved one should have been spared. Share them with a trusted friend, pastor or counselor.

3. Pour out your heart to God, telling God why your loved one's death is so unfair.

Prayer
Lord, we have many questions. It seems so unfair that some die while others live on. From our perspective it all seems random or worse, capricious on your part. We humble ourselves before you, acknowledging that we only see the backside of the tapestry, the broken threads and ugly knots. How all the threads of life and death are woven together, we cannot comprehend. Help us to trust in your love and grace in the midst of our questioning. May we come to find your peace even if we never find answers. Amen.

29 Alzheimer's and Suicide

I have passed out of mind like one who is dead;
I have become like a broken vessel.
For I hear the whispering of many –
terror all around!
Psalm 31:12-13a

When we encounter loss, it complicates whatever other issues we are dealing with in our lives. In our family we were dealing with our daughter's wedding and the mental dementia of my wife's mother when her son, my wife's brother, died by suicide. Mental illness and mental diseases exist in families. When death strikes, our mental disabilities are worsened by the grief. Loss is difficult enough for a healthy mind.

Alzheimer's and a Son's Suicide

In the chapel
I speak
At the pulpit about
My brother-in-law,
Her older son.
I look at Mother sitting
On the front pew to
My left.

147

She is sitting properly
As always
With her daughters, son
Grandchildren.
She looks at me
With empty eyes.

Is Mother's lack of connection
Denial of
Her son's suicide?

Is her distant stare
Progression
Of Alzheimer's
In her brain?

The fog of grief mimics dementia.
Denial of news too hard to take
Parallels damaged cognition.

In the courtyard of the church
Her daughter takes the shovel
Pushes it into the pile of
Gray sandy soil
Lifts dirt over the hole where
The ashes of her brother
Have just been poured.
She turns it over,
Drops the earth
On top of him.

(World
Crushing him
Closing in
Brought him down
To a burnt out hole.)

Her other daughter,

148

I and others
Take our turns
Burying him.

Mother refuses the spade.

Is her mind too weak to
Remember how to grasp a shovel?
Is her heart too broken
For her fingers to wrap
The wooden handle?

Can she not remember
Who her son is, was?
What suicide means?

She recognizes her daughters.
Can she not recall
Her husband's death?
Her father-in-law's suicide
Which she never mentioned?
Does she remember death?
What it means?

What does his death mean?

Is her disconnect because
The reality is too difficult
To grasp?

Has the horrific disease
Protected her from the terrible
Tragedy of her son's decision?

Can she not grieve properly
Because she cannot think right?

How does one grieve properly?

In the receiving line
People are expressing
Heartfelt condolences
At the loss of her son.

At times she seems to recognize
An old friend.
At other times she seems
Completely out of it.

It's awkward.
How do we explain her condition
In front of her
With a momentary
Handshake.
We can't.
We don't
Just thank the people for coming.

Mother sits at the table at the reception
Looking at whoever is speaking.
She eats.
She does not talk.
She does not cry.
She does not question "Why?"
She is lost.
So are we.

I have learned that death comes in the midst of other problems in life. Many times people have to deal with death while trying to face other issues. Death is never a single event but mixed up with all the other aspects of life. Death is never convenient, which complicates our grief. We had our daughter's wedding one Saturday and my wife's brother's memorial service the next Saturday. People die on holidays, when people are away on vacation, when one has that new job interview . . . Death is not a solitary event but tangled in the web of our lives, impacting everything else. My mother-in-law's Alzheimer's brought an extra measure of sadness to her son's suicide and created more issues for my wife, her brother and sister in the midst of their grief.

Encouragement

Part of the difficulty of grief is that it interrupts everything else that is going on. Like a river, life keeps on moving. Even though the dam has given way and the flood has come, you try to do your best. You may wish you could stop everything else in order to deal with your loss. You want to get off the carousel, but it keeps spinning you round and round. You still have to deal with all the other issues from the ordinary to the complex, which were there before your loss. You can only do the best you can under the circumstances. You hope others will understand. You may need to step away from activities and responsibilities as you are able. The more you can delegate, the better.

Important items may fall through the cracks. It happens especially when you are dealing with loss. Months after our son's death I forgot to show up for a class I was to teach. I had never done anything like that before. All I could do was apologize. Taking care of ourselves and those closest to us, is the first order of business in this process of grief. You may not be able to take care of everything else as well as you did before, which may be difficult to accept. You may disappoint some people. Unfortunately that is part of the reality of loss. It's like having an injury while running a marathon. Loss makes you stop to try to deal with the pain while all the other runners are passing you by. You can complete the race even if it takes you longer and you have to limp across the finish line. There you will discover that most of the rest of us came in late and limping as well. Some of us even had to be carried.

Moving Forward

1. Make a "to do" list of the most important things you have to do. By each task write the name of others who could do these things for you. Ask them for help.

2. In light of your loss, see if you can move deadlines for projects further into the future. Ask for extensions wherever you can.

3. Read Exodus 18:13-27 and consider delegating to others.

Prayer

God of grace and glory, may we know your presence with us in the midst of all that is going on in our lives. Help us to continue to take care of the important tasks before us and let go of the less important. Help us to invest ourselves in the relationships that matter most. Please give us discernment, courage and peace. Amen.

30 Dancing to Mourning

The joy of our hearts has ceased; our dancing
has been turned to mourning.
Lamentations 5:15

We were cleaning up after the wedding reception. My daughter and her new husband had just left the fellowship hall for their honeymoon when we got the call. My wife's sister answered her cell phone. She turned to my wife and they fell into each other's arms as the news of their brother's suicide hit them full force.

Wedding Cake and Suicide

The flash flood of grief
Ripped through
The banquet
Of our joy.

Carrying away smiles
Laughter, peace
Tranquility.

The mud of sorrow
Covered all our hopes
Staining the white linens

153

Of our lives.

What gives you the right
To take your own life,
To rob us of one we loved?

Our love was not enough
To keep you from that pain
Or at least to temper it?

Why didn't you get help?
Why couldn't you reach out
To those of us who love you
Who need you?
Why couldn't we reach you?

Your depression
Now saddles each
Of us
Who remain
To mourn your
Murder.

But we cannot
Be judge or jury
To the crime.
Cowardice?
Courage?

You were hurting.
You saw no way out.
A "no show" at the wedding
And ever since.

We will all die. As a pastor I am very aware of that fact. We average a funeral every week or so in our church. A few months ago I officiated at three funerals in one week. On another occasion I had two services on one Saturday. Death often comes at the most inappropriate times. Seldom do we welcome death. I have been with those who have prayed for their loved ones to die, for their suffering to end, but that is the exception. The experience of the sudden and unexpected deaths of my son, my sister and both my brothers-in-law shocked us. Sorrow and sadness flooded our lives where there had been no hint of rain.

So many people are slammed by the news of the death of a loved one. There is no warning, no way to prepare for so many of the losses we experience. Suicide brings its own special horror and pain.

There were suicides in previous generations of our family. No one spoke of them. With suicide a family deals not only with the sudden loss of a loved one but with a heavier load of guilt and shame. We blame ourselves. Shouldn't we have known it was coming? Why didn't we reach out and support them more? What kind of _____ (mother, father, brother, sister, friend) are we that we could not have helped them? We have to work through those emotions and unanswered questions. It is so difficult.

Historically the church has added to that grief by determining suicide was an unforgiveable sin. I can understand the argument logically: Suicide is murdering yourself. Since it is the last act you do, you have no opportunity to repent of that sin, so it remains unforgiven. Jesus opposed such Pharisaic sophistry.

There are actually six suicides reported in the Bible. While all tragic, none of them is condemned for the act itself. Samson (Judges 16:30), Saul and his armor-bearer (1 Samuel 31:4-5), Ahithophel (2 Samuel 17:23), Zimri (1 Kings 16:18), and Judas (Matthew 27:5) all took their lives. The Christian response to suicide should be support of the survivors, not condemnation of the deceased. Jesus commanded us not to judge others but to weep with those who weep.

Encouragement

If you have suffered a suicide among your friends or family, you know tremendous sorrow and loss. There are no words that can cover up the nakedness of that pain. Shame, guilt, and heartbreak are intensified in such grief. It is not your fault. You did not pull the trigger. You did not take the pills.

155

You know that, but that's not how it feels. You feel responsible. You blame yourself. You are angry with them and you are angry with yourself. When someone dies by suicide, we feel that we all have failed. You can get through this. You can be healed. It will take time. No, life will never be the same. Yes, it will always hurt, but you can learn to live with the pain so that life can go on. The anguish will become less intense. The feelings of shame and guilt will subside. You can make it through this.

Moving Forward

1. Seek out a professional counselor if you have experienced a suicide in your family or among your friends. Counselors, psychologists and psychiatrists can be a great help.

2. When you are able, find ways work to promote or work on behalf of suicide prevention.

3. Reflect on John 14:27: *Peace I leave with you; my peace I give to you. I do not give to you as the world gives. Do not let your hearts be troubled, and do not let them be afraid.*

Prayer

God, we do not understand. We blame ourselves. We blame them. Our anger seeks a target. Our shame beats us up. Our guilt overwhelms us. Bring us peace and healing, O Lord. We need you now more than ever. Amen.

FAMILY, FUNERALS AND MEMORIALS

31 My Brother's Keeper

Cain said to his brother Abel, "Let us go out to the field." And when they were in the field, Cain rose up against his brother Abel, and killed him. Then the LORD said to Cain, "Where is your brother Abel?" He said, "I do not know; am I my brother's keeper?"
Genesis 4:8-9

God banished Cain. Adam and Eve were left alone, having lost both of their sons. The editors of the Bible provide an interlude after this loss by focusing on Cain's punishment and his descendants. Then attention is turned back to Adam and Eve with the line, "Adam was intimate with his wife again, and she gave birth to a son and named him Set, saying, 'God has set another offspring for me in place of Abel, because Cain killed him.'" (Gen. 4:25, author's translation) The interlude is a literary device to show the passage of time.

Yes, I know that for many people it's just a story, not to be taken literally. From a literary standpoint the interlude provides time in the story for Adam and Eve to grieve. Yet nothing is said of their grief. Sometimes silence speaks best.

Parents who have lost a child have lots of questions for the couple in our story. How long did it take for Adam and Eve to sleep together after the loss of both sons? Did they come together again in hopes of having another child? Did Eve blame Adam for not being strict enough with Cain, for not controlling him? Did they talk about their loss? Did Adam withdraw emotionally from Eve? Was Eve offended because he was not as emotionally demonstrative as she was after the loss? Did one move on more quickly than the other?

No two people think alike or grieve alike. Losing a child produces incredible stress on a relationship. Many marriages do not survive. Any kind of grief puts pressure on relationships.

A Slow Dance

It's a slow dance, yet
We are never together.
She moves forward
I move back
Trying to match the
Rhythm of this
Mournful music.

She hears a violin
Mourning in a minor key
A mother's lament.

I hear a tenor sax
Wailing a soulful
Father's blues.

Each dances to a different
Slow and painful
Broken heart beat
As we try to
Get through this
Waltz of sadness.

We don't dance through grief.
It dances through us
With a malevolence
That leaves us broken

On the floor.

We don't work through grief.
It works through us
Breaking our hearts
Straining our love
Trying to cut in
To divide us
To take one
Away from the other.

So we hold on
To one another
Moving in
Uncoordinated fashion
Like two sixth graders
At their first dance.

This music of grief
Has made us unsteady
Unsure of ourselves
And each other.

Not knowing how close
To hold each other
What the other needs
Or wants
Because we
Don't know ourselves.

We stumble on
In awkward cadence
Hoping that someday
We will be in step
Together
Again.

Yet how blessed we are
To have a partner

159

In this death dance
Rather than to be
Sidelined
Alone
In the dark
On the side
Of the room
Forgotten
With no one
To hold,
None to
Hold us.

Our experience of grief in the loss of our son helps us understand how some marriages don't last. We have not grieved in the same way at the same time. In the beginning Yvonne was very proactive in seeking out counseling, connecting with a Stephen minister, talking and crying with friends, and reading helpful books. I was amazed at her. It was like she threw herself into her grief.

I could not really talk about the loss of our son, but focused on my work, going back quickly to my 70-hour weeks. She felt forsaken. Eventually I began writing poems early in the morning. I was sobbing by the time I had finished writing. For me, shedding tears while I was alone was healing therapy. We did at times simply hold each other and cry together. We still do on occasion. I was his father. She was his mother. We had two different relationships. We are two different people, who grieve in our own way. We are learning to grieve individually and to grieve together.

Encouragement

If you have a partner in this grief, I encourage you to be patient with each other. Because your relationships with the one you lost are different, because you are two different people with different personalities, and because your individual needs in grief vary from time to time, your grief will be different. Your relationship may feel disjointed, maybe for the first time. You may feel that the other person is not there for you. You may not know how to be

160

there for the other or even want to be there. Grief puts an incredible strain on the relationships of those who survive. Be tolerant of each other's behaviors and expressions of grief, or lack of expression. There is no one way to grieve. There is no right way to grieve.

Moving Forward

1. Make a date with the purpose of talking with each other about your grief. (You may need to do this in a place where you will feel free to cry and hold each other.) In your time together you may find the following questions helpful.

1) What I find most helpful as I go through this grief is:
2) What I need most from you is:
3) How can I be most helpful to you?
4) What am I doing that makes it difficult for you?
5) How can we strengthen our relationship even as we go through this pain?

2. Write a prayer for the other person and share it with them.

3. Take time to pray together in your grief.

4. Read and reflect on 1 Corinthians 13:4-8.

Prayer

Lord, we give you thanks that we are not going through this grief alone. We acknowledge that in our pain we hurt one another. Please forgive us and help us to forgive one another. Aid us in expressing our love for each other even though we ourselves are in pain. Amen.

32 Grandma's Grief

Again, I saw vanity under the sun: the case of solitary individuals, without sons or brothers; yet there is no end to all their toil, and their eyes are never satisfied with riches. "For whom am I toiling," they ask, "and depriving myself of pleasure?" This also is vanity and an unhappy business. Two are better than one, because they have a good reward for their toil. For if they fall, one will lift up the other; but woe to one who is alone and falls and does not have another to help. Again, if two lie together, they keep warm; but how can one keep warm alone? And though one might prevail against another, two will withstand one. A threefold cord is not quickly broken.
Ecclesiastes 4:7-12

Our family was walking out of the church sanctuary, leading the 400 people who had come to share our grief. I turned and saw my parents walking behind me. My mother's knees began to buckle. She was sobbing. I grabbed her arm before she went down., and supported her as we walked to the fellowship hall of the church for the reception.

Grief Tsunami

The earthquake
Of grief
Strikes in the deep

162

Of our ocean
Creating a tsunami
Of sadness
That travels
Fast and far
Flattening those
In its path.

The geography of
Family and friends
Islands located near us
Emotionally
All devastated by
The impact of his death.

The trees he looked up to
Snapped by waves of grief
Broken by the force of loss.

Saplings he had grown up with
Bent to the ground
Twisted by the
Watery weight.

Will they ever
Stand up
Straight again?
His friends
Like cottages along the beach
Forgetting the risk
Splintered into driftwood
Scattered on sand and sea.

Those of us nearest
The epicenter
Have been swept
Out to sea
By this monster wave.

Floating in an
Ocean of despair
Miles from the
Land of life
That was
Before.

One more death,
A drop on the surface
Of the sea of humanity

Yet for those of us
In the path of Poseidon's wrath,
Crushed by this tsunami,
Entire villages
Have been lost.

Legendary hopes drowned
Like Atlantis
Taken by the deep.

"No man is an island," the poet says. I have been greatly encouraged by the hundreds of people who have reached out to us in our grief. We are all connected. The impact of death ripples from parents, siblings, and grandparents to their friends and extended family. As my wife and I grieve, we have watched his sister grieve, his grandparents, his uncles, aunts, and cousins grieve.

We went to California and spent several days with his girlfriend and his best friend, who were devastated. We gathered his friends and co-workers at his house in Lancaster. They were all in mourning. I have learned that, though my grief is overwhelming, it impacts all who loved him and all who love us. The wave of this death, like so many deaths, has altered the landscape of many lives.

Encouragement
As you cannot escape the reality of your own devastation, realize that many others are impacted by this loss. Their

164

connection with you and/or with the one you lost brings sadness to others. Even in your grief you may need to be there to support someone else close to you. Being part of a community, whether it's co-workers, a biological family, or a church congregation, can be a help to you. Your being part of that community is a help to others. At points in the grief process you may need to step back from community for a while. However, as you are able, you will need to come back to friends and family, whom you need and who need you.

Moving Forward

1. Go to family reunions and/or school class reunions as you are able.

2. Attend church services when you are able to do so again.

3. Go out with friends when you are up to it.

4. Allow close friends to bring you a meal and stay to eat with you.

5. Read and reflect on Romans 12:3-8.

Prayer

God you have created us for you and for one another. Help us to allow others to be there for us and help us to be there for others even as we grieve our loss. May we feel your loving presence surrounding us and the presence of that cloud of witnesses, both in heaven and on earth. Amen.

33 Shattered Hearts

A messenger came to Job and said, "The oxen were plowing and the donkeys were feeding beside them, and the Sabeans fell on them and carried them off, and killed the servants with the edge of the sword; I alone have escaped to tell you." While he was still speaking, another came and said, "The fire of God fell from heaven and burned up the sheep and the servants, and consumed them; I alone have escaped to tell you." While he was still speaking, another came and said, "The Chaldeans formed three columns, made a raid on the camels and carried them off, and killed the servants with the edge of the sword; I alone have escaped to tell you." While he was still speaking, another came and said, "Your sons and daughters were eating and drinking wine in their eldest brother's house, and suddenly a great wind came across the desert, struck the four corners of the house, and it fell on the young people, and they are dead; I alone have escaped to tell you."
Job 1:14-19

The biblical character Job was told that his vast holdings of livestock had been stolen or destroyed and that many of his servants had been killed. Wealth was measured in livestock and servants in the ancient world. This was devastating news. Then the fourth messenger brought the worst news of all, "Your children are dead."

My daughter Rebekah Joy called me about 6:15 PM on May 20th, 2013, to tell me our son and her brother, Samuel, had been

166

killed in a motorcycle accident. I left the church immediately to be
with her and my wife.

Where He Breathed His Last

This is where he breathed
His last
On this California canyon road
That he loved to ride.

We pick up pieces
Of his Honda NC 700,
Shards of plastic
Red from the taillight
Gray from the bike's body
Clear from his face shield
Broken shiny steel from the rim
Black rubber tire stem.
Clear glass from the headlight
Scattered at the
Base of the mountain.

This rocky witness
Felt the impact of
His bike and his body
Flinched as it
Let go tears
Of stone onto the road.

We meander among these
Rocky tears as we search
For what?
Evidence of an accident?
Testimony to his love for riding?
Relics of a life lived fast?

No.
In this morbid ritual
We find tender traces of

167

What he had last touched
Where he had last been
Alive,
Where death has scattered
Us all over this sunny road.

Her mother heart lies
Shattered,
Scattered across
The miles of this grief.

Broken into tiny shards
Splintered shrapnel of
Profound love.

I wish that I could help her
Gather those pieces of herself.
But I, too, am shattered and
Scattered and splattered
All across this tearful turn.

And so we walk apart
I on one side of this
Mournful curve
And she on the other.
Stepping around
Mountain tears
Trying to find
Pieces of him
Of her
Of me
Of us.

All the while
Motorcycles
Leaning hard
Roar around this curve
Between us
Reminding us

Of what he loved
And where
He breathed his last.

One of the hardest parts of my experience with grief was to watch the loss devastate my wife and daughter. I wanted to make their grief go away, to ease their pain, to protect them from this terrible loss. I learned I could not do that. I could not fix them any more than I could fix myself. The best I could do was to be there with them, to hold them as we all sobbed together. We had many quivering "group hugs" in those first dark days. At times I had to give them space to grieve alone, just as I needed alone time. I learned that no two people grieve in the same way. I learned to be more patient with them and with myself. I am still learning.

At weddings I have often shared that the companionship in marriage means that joys are doubled and sadness is halved. Many pastors say something like that. I no longer say that the companionship of a spouse can cut sorrows in half.

Why? Because while it was a tremendous comfort for me to have my wife with me as we endured this pain together, watching her grieve nearly killed me. I now tell couples they can lean on one another during difficult times, which I hope will be true for them.

Encouragement

Watching other family members or friends grieve a loss as you are going through it adds to the suffering of grief. When you hear them crying, you begin to cry. You lie in bed not sleeping, listening to them softly sobbing, tossing and turning. You want to take away their pain, to help them, to ease their suffering. You are powerless to help. We all are. There is nothing you can say or do that is going to make it hurt less. The best you can do is be there for each other with as much patience, kindness, and caring as you can muster.

Moving Forward

1. Write a note to those who share your grief telling them how much you appreciate their being a part of your life in this struggle and that you will be there for them as best you can.

2. Call someone you know who is struggling with this loss—just to touch base, to listen, and to talk.

3. Read and reflect on Romans 12:9-18.

Prayer
Lord, you have called us to love one another. When death comes, we need each other even more. Help us to be present for others. Enable us to be honest with our own grief and patient and loving with others as they grieve. Amen.

34 Lost World

Some Sadducees, those who say there is no resurrection, came to him and asked him a question, "Teacher, Moses wrote for us that if a man's brother dies, leaving a wife but no children, the man shall marry the widow and raise up children for his brother. Now there were seven brothers; the first married, and died childless; then the second and the third married her, and so in the same way all seven died childless. Finally the woman also died. In the resurrection, therefore, whose wife will the woman be? For the seven had married her.

Jesus said to them, "Those who belong to this age marry and are given in marriage; but those who are considered worthy of a place in that age and in the resurrection from the dead neither marry nor are given in marriage. Indeed they cannot die anymore, because they are like angels and are children of God, being children of the resurrection."
Luke 20:27-36

A young woman had lost her husband two weeks before and was missing him terribly. She asked me about being with him in heaven. She said, "I want to be with him. How can we be together? How does that work? If a person has been married to more than one person what will happen?" Her husband had been married previously.

I said, "The Sadducees asked Jesus a similar question." But their agenda was to trip Jesus up regarding his view of the resurrection. I went on, "I see heaven as a place of love. God is

171

love. Heaven must be filled with love. How can your love for a person you have loved here be any less in heaven? How could their love for you be any less? Your love for each other can only be more—multiplied because you are in the presence of ultimate love." She was comforted. I had actually never formulated an answer to that question until that moment. It seemed the right answer to me then and still does today.

The Lost World

I lost my wedding ring
On a softball field
Hours with a metal
Detector could not
Discover.

I lost my son
To a motorcycle
Crash
Gone forever.

Love gone
Love done
Love lost.

In our Humpty Dumpty
World
The pieces never fit
Back together again.
If we could
Even find them.

But You live in
That world of love
Where nothing is lost
All is gain.

Lost love
Deepens my grief

In this lost world.

All the love
We had
I have
You have
Is multiplied there.

What withers here
By death and dying,
What fades upon
The page of ancient lines

Is indelibly written
In bold
In the book of life
In that land of love
Eternal.

We have many questions about the afterlife. Some people think they have it all nailed down, like the Sadducees in Jesus' day who denied eternity or the Pharisees who had their theology of the afterlife all worked out. The loss of our son made me question everything in my theology, including my views of heaven and hell.

In our church we have had a class for those who are grieving. In one of the later sessions this video series addressed the question, "What if your loved one is not in heaven?" That offended me for at least three reasons. First, it is a terrible question to raise for those who are grieving, who are already filled with troubling questions of their own. When I first saw it, I complained, "This series is supposed to be comforting!"

Second, the question assumes we can know which people are accepted by God into eternity and which are not. Their answer was even worse: "You will be so filled with joy in heaven, you won't care that your loved one is not there with you." Seriously?

Third, the question implies a God whose ultimate goal is not love or comfort, but judgment and condemnation, at least for some. In this thinking, God excludes the vast majority of people and accepts a select few for eternal life.

I prefer to see God in the practice of Jesus who included everyone, especially those deemed unworthy, in his circle of friends — traitors, prostitutes, the religious elite, greedy businessmen, smelly fishermen and rebels. Jesus did not exclude anyone. He even accepted Judas. If that is how Jesus lived and if we believe Jesus is God in the flesh, how can we be so certain God becomes exclusive in the afterlife? Jesus went to be with those most in need of grace.

There are passages in the New Testament about ultimate judgment. The criteria for those excluded from heaven includes the following: not believing in Jesus (John 3:18), not forgiving others (Matt. 6:14-15), not keeping the commandments (Luke 18:18-22), not visiting people in prison (Matt. 25:43), not giving all to the poor (Luke 18:22), not loving one's neighbor as oneself (Luke 10:27-28), and not feeding the hungry (Matt. 25:42). One will also be excluded for premarital sex, anger, jealousy, quarreling, envy, and getting drunk, among other things (Gal. 5:19-20). Jesus offered grace to people guilty of making mistakes, as he did to the woman caught in the act of adultery (John 8:3-11). Does Jesus change in the afterlife?

I have not worked out the answers to all these questions. These and other questions help me to realize we don't have all the answers about this life or the next. When it comes to the afterlife in particular, we all need to be humble about our opinions. As a grieving pastor, all I can do is offer my love to others who are grieving and point to God's love for each one of us.

Encouragement

If you are like most people, you believe in an afterlife. Part of the grief process involves questioning everything. What will happen to my loved one in the afterlife? Will I join them when I die? What will it be like? Only God knows what will happen to any of us after we die. Only the Lord and those who have already died could tell us what that world is like.

I encourage you to have confidence in a God who loves us in spite of our shortcomings in this life and who loves us into the next. If you encounter people who portray the Christian God as judgmental, ask yourself if that is the God revealed in Jesus Christ. Remember that they do not have the full picture of God. None of us does.

Moving Forward

1. Read the following from Luke's crucifixion scene:

> *One of the criminals who were hanged there kept deriding him and saying, "Are you not the Messiah? Save yourself and us!" But the other rebuked him, saying, "Do you not fear God, since you are under the same sentence of condemnation? And we indeed have been condemned justly, for we are getting what we deserve for our deeds, but this man has done nothing wrong." Then he said, "Jesus, remember me when you come into your kingdom." He replied, "Truly I tell you, today you will be with me in Paradise."*
> (Luke 23:39-43)

2. Imagine the scene when you greet your loved ones in heaven. What would you say to them? What do you think they will say to you?

Prayer

God of all grace, help us to believe in your goodness and mercy even when we don't understand. Help us to have confidence that you love the one we lost and that you love us. We commit ourselves and the ones we love to your care in this life and the next, good and loving Shepherd. Amen.

35 What Kind of Service?

I will turn your feasts into mourning,
and all your songs into lamentation;
I will bring sackcloth on all loins,
and baldness on every head;
I will make it like the mourning for an only son,
and the end of it like a bitter day.
Amos 8:10

Speaking for God, the prophet Amos threatened destruction of the people of Israel for their mistreatment of the poor, cruelty to the marginalized, deceitful business practices, and turning away from God. Amos promised that when the enemy conquered Israel, the people would experience the worst kind of sorrow, which he likened to "the mourning for an only son." How do we observe the death of a child, a spouse, a parent, a sibling or a friend? What do we do when a person we love dies? Should we have a service?

That is one of the many questions that comes up when you experience the death of a loved one. In Amos' day, instead of feasting together people would come together to mourn. Instead of happy songs people would sing laments and wail as they buried the body of their loved one.

Communities still gather around those who have suffered loss as they have for millennia. Specific traditions vary, such as putting on sackcloth and pouring ashes on one's head.

Some people tell their loved ones that they do not want a funeral or memorial service after their death. Most people observe those wishes. As a pastor, I have been invited many times to "say a few words" at a grave with only family present. Once I held a service at a grave with only four family members. More often, people have a funeral or memorial service in a funeral home or in a church and open it up to family and friends.

No Service for Me

You know, Dad,
I would not want
A service.

Don't say anything
About me.

Nothing to a crowd
Nothing religious
Nothing sentimental
Nothing to make Mom cry.

No service for me, Dad,
Please.

Sorry, Son
It's what people do.
It was because of you
That we gathered together
To honor you
To remember you
To celebrate you
To grieve over you.

We needed to be
With friends
Who did not
Know you,
Friends who did.

177

Our family needed
To grieve your loss
Together.

We needed to
Affirm our faith
In God.
To hold on to the hope
Of resurrection,
Of eternal life.

Your friends needed
To come together
To honor you
To remember you
To celebrate you
To grieve over you.

I apologize
For not doing
What you wanted.

Our love for you
Forced gathering with
Our community
And yours
Our God
And yours.

Our love for you
Made us grieve
Made us remember
Made us take time to honor you
Made us celebrate your life
Through our tears.

There was no question that we would have a service for our son. As a pastor, I have seen the value of a community embracing those who grieve. Our church family encircled us with their love. They loved us beyond our expectations. We needed their compassion.

In a church I served in Miami, a German lady, who had moved to Miami with her husband before WWII, was a long time member. When she died, her three daughters, who lived in different parts of the U.S., came to take care of arrangements. They were not religious. All three were adamant they did not want a service of any kind.

The German lady's friends wanted a service to remember her. Her best friend convinced the daughters to allow a service in her honor. I met with them and planned the service. After the reception, all three daughters thanked her best friend and me several times. Why? Because they had learned from their mother's friends and community how important she was to them. They heard how loving and kind she had been. They felt the love of this church family, not only for their mother but also for them. It was a step toward healing. The service turned out to be a meaningful and helpful time for them.

On June 1, 2013, twelve days after our son's death, we held a memorial service at Plantation United Methodist Church, where I was serving as senior pastor. About four hundred people came. Only about 30 of them had ever met my son.

Three weeks later, we gathered his friends at his home in Lancaster, California, for a time of remembering. It was not a service in the traditional sense. His best friend, girlfriend, and her family came. My son would have been happy with his motorcycle courier buddies who rode up from Los Angeles to his house. They left a space on the street for his missing motorcycle as they lined theirs up. My daughter's good friend came from San Diego with her husband and kids. There were about 30 of us all together. All of us knew my son. It was an important time for us to hear stories from his friends.

Encouragement

Gathering with family and friends is important. Whether in a formal service or informally, I would encourage you to spend time together. Even though you may want to crawl in a hole and not deal with anyone, it is good to be with those who love you. It may be one of the most difficult days of your life, to participate in a service for a loved one, but it is important for healing and for the grief process. If you cannot gather with others, those who love you will understand.

If you want to respect the wishes of a loved one who was opposed to having a service, that is a way of honoring them. Having a service or not having one is up to you. There is no right or wrong. In a time when you can barely think, having to plan details of a service is another burden, but it may be important for you to do that. Get the help of others as you make these decisions.

Moving Forward

1. If you have not had a service, contact a pastor, priest, or funeral home to plan a service.

2. Take a friend and/or key family members with you when you go to meet with the funeral director, priest or pastor.

3. If you did not have a service but would like to honor your loved one, a memorial service can be planned for any time after one has passed. You could even plan a service on the anniversary of your loved one's passing.

4. Read and reflect on Lamentations 2:10-11.

Prayer

Lord, guide us in all our decisions, especially in the important decision of how to honor and remember the one we lost. Help us to do what brings the most meaning and healing into our lives. If we have a service, carry us through those heartbreaking hours, which can seem like days. Amen.

36 Ashes to Ashes

So it is with the resurrection of the dead. What is sown is perishable, what is raised is imperishable. It is sown in dishonor, it is raised in glory. It is sown in weakness, it is raised in power. It is sown a physical body, it is raised a spiritual body.
I Corinthians 15:42-44a

Is it wrong to cremate someone? For centuries Christians opposed cremation. Why? The New Testament talks about the bodily resurrection of Jesus Christ. The hope presented there is that we Christians will also be resurrected in bodily form. How that will happen exactly is difficult to discern. St. Paul talked about the kernel or seed of the body being buried and then raised to a new body (1 Cor. 15:35-58).

Burial was the custom of ancient Jews and so also of Christians. They were actually countercultural in the ancient world because in Greece and Rome cremation was the norm. Christians buried their dead in catacombs. They thought that to voluntarily burn someone's remains would be to desecrate what God was going to raise. They reserved burning bodies for witches and heretics.

Modern cremation began to gain ground in Europe in the late 1800's prompting the Roman Catholic Church to ban cremation in 1886. The ban was lifted in 1983, although burial was and is still the recommendation of the Roman Catholic Church, as it is of the Greek Orthodox Church.

A Methodist asked me last week, "If you are cremated, does that mean you will not go to heaven?" My response was similar to Paul's approach to keeping the Sabbath or eating meat sacrificed to idols in Romans: "Let all be fully convinced in their own minds." (Romans 14:5b)

I see nothing wrong with cremation. When the dead are raised, if God needs to put our molecules back together again, God can do so whether they have been burned or decomposed in the dirt or salt water. I tell people that I am planning to be cremated. That has shocked a few parishioners over the years. For me, this is a personal or family decision. There are practical pros and cons to cremation just as there is for burial.

My son and I had talked about many things. But we did not talk about what to do with his remains if he died. We decided to have him cremated.

Dividing Your Ashes

I don't know
If you would approve
Being burned or
That we divided
Your ashes.

Your mother and sister
Spread some of you
From heights in Yosemite.

You were supposed to be with us
On that trip.
Our first family vacation in years.
So they took your ashes along.

You were killed a few weeks
Before we arrived to take you
On vacation.
You were so excited
You could not sleep.

No, we did not make it
To the Grand Canyon
No ashes there, yet.
We were busy
Hosting your friends
For a celebration of your life.
Then your ashes
Were all together
In a pretty cylindrical
Cardboard box
With a sunset on it.

Your mom and sister
Spread part of
Your remains
At Vanderbilt Beach
Where you loved to go
To celebrate your birthday.

Your girlfriend Martiza
Took some of you.
As did your best friend Matt.
He made an urn for
You out of wood.
It is beautiful!

I had no desire to spread
Your ashes,
Panicked
At the thought of not having
Any part of you
For myself.

Weird that
Your ashes
Lie in a box on my dresser

Your photo is on top,
You in your black leather jacket

Leaning on
Your black Honda Shadow.

I don't know if you
Care at all
What we have done
With what is left of you.

Rebekah and Maritza
Have a little bit of your ashes
In lockets around their necks.

A friend of ours
Who lost her son
Three days
Before the anniversary
Of your death
Wanted some of you
For a locket for Yvonne.
A surprise.

I measured out
A teaspoon of you.

Every speck of
You is precious to me.

I lament you
Are spread from the
California mountains
To the beaches of Florida,
Ashes in lockets
Ashes in jewelry boxes.

Maybe that's what
You would prefer
Than to gather dust
On my dresser.

The nursery rhyme
We used to read you
Echoes like a diabolical dirge
"All the king's horses
And all the king's men
Could not put him back
Together again."

I wish you were whole
Not broken
Not burned
Not scattered

Me too.

I am learning to live with our decisions regarding our son's death. We did not fly out to California to see his broken body. We had him cremated in the town where he lived. We do not know if he would have wanted that.

Friends of ours lost their son in his late teens. They buried him in South Florida where he died and where they had lived for decades. They retired and decided to move to the other side of the country to be near their surviving child and their grandchildren. But they did not want to leave their son back in Florida so they looked into having his remains dug up and transported to the west and reburied. It was so costly they could not afford it. Is there a good way to handle the remains of a loved one?

Encouragement

Perhaps you had to decide whether to bury your mother by her first or second husband. Perhaps you went with cremation because it was cheaper. Even if the deceased's wishes are known, it is a difficult decision to have to make about their remains, especially when the fog of grief clouds our judgment. When we do not know what they would have wanted, it seems even more traumatic. We may not get to decide what will happen with their bodies, which adds to grief.

If possible, we should make our wishes known to others. Families often struggle to come to an agreement. God's grace covers all our decisions, whether we regret them later or not. We do the best we can at the moment when forced to make choices. Part of your grieving is learning to live with the new normal, which also includes making final arrangements for your loved one and living with those decisions.

Moving Forward

1. Watch a DVD or slideshow of your loved one with family and friends.

2. Visit the grave. Say a prayer. Sit down by the grave. Put flowers there. Stretch out on the grass—whatever helps.

3. Hold your loved one's ashes in your hands while giving thanks to God for this person's life and praying to God for strength.

4. Read and reflect on 1 Corinthians15:35-58.

Prayer

Lord, we clergy often say, "ashes to ashes, dust to dust." We acknowledge that our lives have an end. Only you are eternal, O God. We are finite. When we lose someone we love, we so often do not know what is right, what we should do for them or for ourselves. Give us your wisdom to make the right choices and your grace to live with the choices we have made. Amen.

37 We Wore Bright Colors

Then the LORD God formed man from the dust of the ground, and breathed into his nostrils the breath of life; and the man became a living being. And the LORD God planted a garden in Eden, in the east; and there he put the man whom he had formed. Out of the ground the LORD God made to grow every tree that is pleasant to the sight and good for food, the tree of life also in the midst of the garden, and the tree of the knowledge of good and evil.
Genesis 2:7-9

So out of the ground the LORD God formed every animal of the field and every bird of the air, and brought them to the man to see what he would call them; and whatever the man called every living creature, that was its name.
Genesis 2:19

Plants and animals figure prominently in our lives. When people die it affects the world around them, not only the people but other creatures as well. Our son loved plants and animals. People were often more difficult for him.

Billy Buttons Mourns

They had all died,
All the plants
That filled your

187

Backyard
Which had turned
Into desert.

They died
Because the
One who had
Planted them
Watered them
Cared for them
Was gone.

We tried to
Save your
Apple trees.

Your dog
Billy Buttons
Your Lab/Shepherd/Wolf
Friend
Lay by the front door
For three days
After your death.

He refused to eat.
He refused to budge.
Waiting
Whimpering
Whining,
He mourned
The death of
His best friend
His constant companion.

You were a daddy to him.
He did not understand
Why you never returned.
He waited for days.

Weeks later when
He jumped in your truck
For the first time
Since you left,
He went crazy.

Picked up your scent,
Knew you were there
Got so excited.
Looked everywhere.
Then lay down in your
Driver's seat.

Billy Buttons still mourns.

His sister put the word out. Our son, her brother, so tough on the outside, liked flowers. Our motorcycle-riding daredevil liked to raise plants as a hobby. So we did not wear black at his memorial service. Everyone wore bright colors at his service. I wore a bright blue shirt. Blue was his favorite color. My dad was dressed in a bright yellow shirt. My mom and daughter wore floral prints. My wife wore purple. Like many funerals and memorials, it was to be a celebration of life.

We had to make decisions about his truck, his house, his dog, his books, and his old motorcycle (the new one was a total loss). I would have taken his dog, but his girlfriend took Billy in. His best friend tried to save the apple trees my son had planted weeks before. We did the best we could to take care of the things that mattered to him, including his dog, his plants, and his house. Like him, some could not be saved.

Encouragement
When you lose someone you love, what mattered to that person may become an issue. The things may matter to you, especially now. If your loved one had a will, it may help with legal matters regarding property. However, the practical issues of dealing with possessions and passions may present problems for you. Not being the one who makes decisions about the belongings may complicate the grieving process for you.

189

On the other hand, being the one who decides can be very difficult. You may be angry that now you have to deal with these things. You may feel you let your loved one down by decisions you make. The hardest part may be dealing with pets, who were like family to your loved one. Some people's lives are blessed because they can adopt the pet that was left. Others cannot and have to let go of their loved one's cat, dog, parrot, horse, or other pet. Either way it can add to your sense of loss. As you make decisions about what mattered to your loved one, know that you matter to God. God's grace and love surrounds you during this difficult time.

Moving Forward

1. See an attorney regarding your loved one's estate.

2. Involve those closest to him or her or someone you trust to help you make decisions about the possessions left behind.

3. If there is no legal claim on personal or other items, make a list. Beside each item list the name of the person whom you think your loved one would want to have it.

4. If you cannot take care of your loved one's pet, consider family members or friends who might enjoy the pet. If you cannot find someone to adopt the pet, take it to a humane shelter, which adopts out animals and does not euthanize them.

5. Give plants to someone who knew your loved one and who also loves plants.

6. Read and reflect on Isaiah 11:6-9.

Prayer

God of all creation, you created life but death comes to us. We pray that as we sort out the pieces of our loved one's life, you would guide us. Help us deal with the emotions of sadness and guilt. Clarify our thinking in this fog of grief. We need your help. Amen.

38 How Long, O Lord?

*The Israelites wept for Moses in the plains of Moab thirty days; then the
period of mourning for Moses was ended.*
Deuteronomy 34:8

*O LORD God of hosts,
how long will you be angry with your people's prayers?
You have fed them with the bread of tears,
and given them tears to drink in full measure.*
Psalm 80:4-5

It's good that some companies offer three days paid bereavement.
That gives time to take off to be with the family for a funeral or
memorial service. But is three days long enough to finish
mourning? How long does it take before we can function well
again? What role does work play in our time of grief?

Tomb Time

That's it.
Three Days.
It's all the time
We get off work,
To mourn.

That's more
Than some.

Three days.

Tomb time
For Lazarus
For Jesus.

They were
Released.
We remain shackled,
Bound in the dark,
Wrapped in
Grave clothes.

Back on the job
We pretend
To walk in the light,
Stumbling along
Tripping over
Tombstones
Crashing our
Hearts into daily
Routines.

It's what is expected.
The great pretense
That life goes on
Except it doesn't.

We go through
The motions
Of normality
When all has changed.

Many employers
Expect you
To show up

The next day or
After three days.
Sure you can use
Vacation time--
If you need it.

I did.
I needed more
Time to be with
My surviving loves,
My wife
My daughter.

Time to collect
His ashes
Across the country
Time to plan services.
Time to meet with
His friends.
Time to weep.

Yes, I did go back
Too soon.
Many of us do.

Medical Leave Act
Grants leave to care
For an ailing
Family member
For those who qualify —
Twelve weeks.

When they die.
Time's up.
Almost.

Jewish tradition
Grants the family
Seven days, sitting Shiva.

Others insist on a month off
For the death of a spouse or
The loss of a child.

In times past
Widows were expected
To wear black for a year.

In our workaholic
World where
Production equals worth
Three days
Bereavement pay
Seems a generous
Concession.

The mare and stallion
Pulled together for years.
Their colt and filly
Destined to pull the
Wagon and plow behind them.
Then their colt was killed.

The next morning
The farmer came to
Harness his team.
"Sorry for your loss."
He mocked his own horses.

The stallion trudged out of
The open stall door
Submitting to the
Yoke of work.

The mare refused
To budge.
No amount of pulling
Whipping or punching

Could persuade her
Mother's heart to beat
For any other purpose
Than to mourn
Her offspring.

The nearly grown filly
Hesitated to leave
The comforting dark.

She finally stepped out
Joined her father
In the oppressive light.

They bowed their heads to the
Farmer's yoke to plow
His field and salt the
Ground with their tears.

"Horses were made to work!"
The farmer yelled
As he slapped the reins
On the glistening backs
Of his sluggish mourners.

Are we?

I'm a workaholic. I confess. I needed to work soon after the loss of our son. At the same time, I needed not to work. For me, working was my salvation and my torment. Two months after our son's service I met with the parents of our beloved nursery worker, who had died unexpectedly at 34 years old. I tried to comfort them. During the service I shared words about their loss from my own experience, fighting back tears. From the pulpit I saw them weeping where my wife and I had cried on the front pew by the center aisle.

Over the next 16 months as a pastor I attempted to comfort the family of a 38-year-old man who died suddenly, our Youth Director and his wife in the loss of their stillborn daughter, the

195

parents of a 39-year-old son, our sister and brother-in-law in the sudden death of our 36-year-old nephew, our best friends in the loss of their 47-year-old son, parents of a 36-year-old son who died in his sleep, parents of an 18-year-old daughter, as well as other families whose loved ones died at more "normal" ages. I am a pastor. It's what I do. It's who I am.

We left the emergency room where my wife and I had offered comfort to our friend, a grieving mother whose son had unexpectedly died in his sleep hours before. It was our son's birthday. As we were walking to the car, my wife said to me, "You've got to find another line of work." For both of us it felt like piling one grief on another was going to bury us alive. On the other hand, our having survived the loss of our son seemed to help grieving families see that they could get through this. They knew that we understood their pain.

Encouragement

You may have had to return to your work while your heart is still broken. You may have difficulty concentrating on actions that you normally do without a second thought. You may be making mistakes. The fog of grief makes it impossible to function normally. Whether you have your own business, work for someone else, or are retired, grief disturbs your ability to think and affects how well you can perform routine jobs, let alone difficult projects. For a period of time you may have to step back from responsibilities for your own sake and the sake of others. Do not think less of yourself for having these problems. It's a normal aspect of grief. Allow yourself some grace and be willing to accept grace from others.

Moving Forward

1. Make a list of the tasks that you are facing. By each task write "D" for delegate, "H" for help, or "P" for postpone. By the letter "D" write a name of someone to whom you can delegate the job. By the letter "H" write a person's name who can help you complete the task. Postpone as many things as you can. Do the best you can with the remaining items. Keep adding to this list and crossing off things as you do them. If making this list is too difficult, ask a friend or family member to help you work through

it. This may give you peace of mind and a sense of control in your emotional turmoil.

2. If you need to take more time off work, make an appointment to talk to your supervisor to see what you can arrange.

3. If you are self-employed, look for creative ways to bring in others to handle different aspects of your work. Defer and postpone as much as you can while you take time to grieve.

4. Read and reflect on Psalm 13.

Prayer
O Lord, in the story of Adam and Eve you put them to work tending the Garden of Eden. Our work is a gift from you. In our grief we find it difficult to continue to do. When we cannot function, allow us to take Sabbath time to rest, to grieve, and to heal. When we cannot do, help us to be, to rest in your arms. Amen.

LIVING WITH THE NEW NORMAL

39 Senior No More?

Adam knew his wife again, and she bore a son and named him Seth, for she said, "God has appointed for me another child instead of Abel, because Cain killed him."
Gen. 4:25

This is the list of the descendants of Adam. When God created humankind, he made them in the likeness of God. Male and female he created them, and he blessed them and named them "Humankind" when they were created. When Adam had lived one hundred thirty years, he became the father of a son in his likeness, according to his image, and named him Seth.
Genesis 5:1-3

Seth is Adam and Eve's third son. Their firstborn, Cain, killed the younger Abel, out of jealousy. The first parents had to suffer the loss of a child, really two children. Abel was murdered by Cain, who was banished. Fratricide would have to be a parent's worst nightmare.

Before we lost our son, I never gave it much thought that the first biblical parents had lost a child to death. There in the first chapters of the Bible we encounter the deepest grief imaginable. So many parents throughout history have suffered the loss of a child--from Adam and Eve to David and Bathsheba to Joseph and Mary, from Mr. & Mrs. Abraham Lincoln to Mr. & Mrs. Martin Luther King, Sr. While every grief is difficult, losing a child has its own special burden.

Ode to Former "Seniors"

What did we do
To obtain the
Honorary degree
Of Sr.?

We fathered a son
Born in our image
And in our likeness
Named our name.

We created a Junior
Who might not
Be at all like us
Or might be the
"Spittin' image."

He learned to walk
Like us
Talk like us
Think like us.

Or perhaps he rebelled
Against the name
That made him
A shadow of us.

Mine did rebel
Against having a preacher Dad.
Claiming atheism
Doing whatever a
Preacher's kid
Should not.

What do we do now
That Junior has died?
Do we drop the Sr.
After our names?

Would that be denying
That we ever had a son
Who was given our name?

Do we bury that
Honorary title
Like we buried him?
Or cremate "Sr."?

Do we drop the abbreviation
Because his life was shortened
Ending before ours?
Seniors are supposed to die
Before Juniors.

I grieve every time
I write "Sr." after my name.

But if I leave it off
I deny a part of me,
The best part of me
That existed.

Do I keep writing "Sr."
As a confession
That I did not protect
Him as a father ought
To protect a son?

Is writing "Sr." like
Wearing a cross
Around my neck
Acknowledging the death

Of my son
Who died at the same age
As Jesus?

After the resurrection
Is it still God, the Father,
God, Sr.
And God, the Son,
God, Jr.?
Or are they now
A Mystery of One?

When I die
Will I get to be with my Jr.?
Will they say when I arrive
"Hey Samuel, Jr.
Your Dad walks,
Talks just like
You"?

Will I be the Jr.
And he the Sr.
Because he arrived
Before I did?

Will I be his Dad
Any longer?
All the more reason
To hang on to "Sr."

Though not a legal
Part of my name,
Our bond goes beyond
Legalities.

Our Jr./Sr. connection
Now broken
But never
Forgotten.

I remain
Samuel Lee Wright, Sr.

My son's legal name was Samuel Lee Wright, Jr. My grandmother was upset with me that we did not name him Samuel Lee Wright, III. I was named after my grandfather by the same name, so my son should have been "the Third" according to her argument.

I actually did not want to name him after me. That is what my wife, Yvonne, wanted. In the end, I could not resist such an honor—to have a son named after me? While Jr. was legally part of my son's name, Sr. was added to mine only when my son was born. Sr. lets others know that I have a son by the same name. But what about now that he has died?

Encouragement

Things will never be the same. The loss of a child, a spouse, a parent, a brother, or sister, changes one's life forever. You will adjust to this new reality. It will take time, much time. With the help of God and others, you will make it.

Moving Forward

1. Have your favorite photo of your loved one enlarged. Hang it in a prominent place in your home.

2. Have your loved one's name engraved on a plaque and place it by a favorite tree.

3. Get a new collar engraved for your loved one's pet with the person's name on it, for example, "Billy, Samuel's dog."

4. Read and reflect on Psalm 27.

Prayer

God bless all who mourn the loss of a loved one, whatever their relationship. Be with all of us parents who have lost children and grieve this bitterness, including us Seniors. Amen.

40 Don't Leave Home Without It!

I am weary with my moaning;
every night I flood my bed with tears;
I drench my couch with my weeping.
My eyes waste away because of grief.
Psalm 6:6-7a

Don't Leave Home Without It! That was the tag line of a credit card commercial. It's impossible to leave grief behind.

Our youth mission team went to Costa Rica to do some painting and repair of a building at the Methodist Center in Alajuela. We were painting 16 dorm rooms and 5 bathrooms on the second floor that had been neglected for years. Heladio was the man in charge of the facility. He initially gave us sandpaper, scrapers, ladders, and spackling. Under his guidance, our youth and adults got busy with prep work in different rooms. He was very grateful for our help.

In my broken Spanish I asked him if he had children. He said he had two boys, one in heaven and one here. His son in heaven died as he was crossing the street at his school, hit by a car nine years before. He was only nine years old. Heladio said he cried for a year. I told him our son had died in a motorcycle accident a year before. We bonded as only fathers who have lost children can. Tears came to my eyes. Heladio put his hand on my shoulder. We both agreed that only God can heal broken hearts.

The Baggage of Grief

My wife sits in the middle
While I man the aisle.
The Cuban woman
Sits next to her
By the window.
My wife's grief spills out
For a moment.

She tells the woman we are
Flying to California
To pick up our son's ashes.

The woman acknowledges
This is her fifth
Annual pilgrimage flight
To Los Angeles where
Her son died also.

You can't leave grief behind.

We get on a plane
To Istanbul
Did not check
The bag of grief
But it is there waiting for us
Oversize and overweight
But there is no charge.

We board a ship
Bound for Greece.
We dock in Santorini.
While others are taking in the sites
On this beautiful Greek island,
Yvonne and I
Are lighting candles
In a Greek Orthodox Church

Then in a Roman Catholic Church
Remembering our son.

Grief takes no holiday.

In conversations with strangers
About our families
I dread the question
"Do you have children?"

What should I say?
"Yes I have a daughter."
Should I remain silent,
Deny our son existed?

"One now. Used to have two."
Or do I admit this weight of grief
Let them weigh it on the scale
And pay the penalty
For grief to ride along with us.

Do I attempt to shove grief
Beneath the seat
Pretending it does not
Count
It does not weigh
Me down?

Would that I
Could so easily move these
Ingots of lead shackled to
My ankles.

When courage flashes
Through my mind
And I show my burden
To others
I find
In every row of the plane

205

Every pew of the church
Every table in the restaurant
Others carrying
Bags that match mine.

I would much rather leave this grief behind me. But it has become part of who I am, like someone missing a limb. I cannot change what has happened. Nor can I pretend it did not happen. "Don't Leave Home Without It!" Do we have a choice?

Encouragement

You have to carry your burden of grief any way you can. You may find that suffering in silence works best for you. You may want to share with others what happened. You may do either or both depending on the day. You will find others who pretend they have no grief. Perhaps they really do not yet carry this burden of sorrow. If you open up to others, you may be surprised how many have suffered loss. You are not alone in grief.

Moving Forward

1. Join a support group for those who have suffered loss.

2. Attend a class, such as GriefShare to walk with others in your grief.

3. Find a church that has a Stephen Ministry and ask for a Stephen Minister.

4. Read the lyrics to the Gospel song, "Precious Lord, Take My Hand." Sing it if you can.

Prayer

O God, how long must I carry this heavy burden of grief? How long must I bear this weight? Help me to manage this load of sorrow. If my sharing helps others carry their grief, let the words stumble out so that we can carry the burden together. Whether I remain silent or speak, may your grace carry both me and my loss through this day. Amen.

41 The New Normal

*Now his [Eli's] daughter-in-law, the wife of Phinehas, was pregnant,
about to give birth. When she heard the news that the ark of God was
captured, and that her father-in-law and her husband were dead, she
bowed and gave birth; for her labor pains overwhelmed her. As she was
about to die, the women attending her said to her, "Do not be afraid, for
you have borne a son." But she did not answer or give heed. She named
the child Ichabod, meaning, "The glory has departed from Israel,"
because the ark of God had been captured and because of her father-in-
law and her husband. She said, "The glory has departed from Israel, for
the ark of God has been captured."*
1 Samuel 4:19-22

This passage tells about a dark moment in Israel's history when
Eli, the high priest, died at hearing about the death of his two sons
and the enemy capture of the ark of God. Then his daughter-in-
law went into labor the moment she learned of the death of her
husband, father-in-law, and brother-in-law. She died in childbirth.
Before she breathed her last, she named the child Ichabod, "No
Glory," because God's glory and presence had departed from
Israel. What a horrible name to give a child. Yet the name
described Israel's new normal in that era. Your loss may make you
feel like all the goodness and glory of life has abandoned you.

207

The New Normal

Is this what it feels like
To lose a leg
Or an arm?
It's lost,
Gone forever.
Things will never
Be the same.

Death has stolen
Part of me
And not just a little
But a limb
Or a lung
Or a heart.

People may expect me
To be back to normal
But normal has changed.
I'm not back to it.
Never will be.
Nor up to this
New reality
Not yet.

How long does it take
To function normally
After the death of a spouse,
A daughter or a son?
A year? Two?

We long
To sleep through
The night again.
To wake without
Tears flowing.

To buy groceries

Without grabbing the wrong can,
Picking up flour instead of sugar,
Not forgetting what is on
The list
In our hand.

Will the new normal
Mean we can think
Like before
Instead of reading
The same paragraph
Three times
Without knowing
What it says?

We return to
Doing normal
Long before
We are ready.

We bump along
In the dark
On our way
To the new normal.

Will the new
Be worth living?
Will I want to stay there?
Will people stare
Because
I am missing part of me?
Or is that only clear to me
That I am not whole
Nor will I ever be?

A massive sink hole
Has swallowed
The living room
Of my heart

Leaving a gaping
Mouth to the
Abyss where
He has gone.
I barely escape
Being swallowed
With the loss.

Though there is
Room to walk
Around the darkness,
For weeks
I dangled my feet
Sitting on the edge
Leaning toward the hungry dark
Wondering if it would not be better
If it swallowed me too.

Now I only pause to look
Into the deep
As I step carefully
Around the massive
Wound at the center
Of my heart.

What's gone is gone
Never to be replaced.
I can't regrow
What's amputated.
I can't fill in
This black hole.

Time drags me
By the hair
On our way
To the new normal.

Grief made me feel like God's presence had departed from my life. I entered into the "dark night of the soul," which many have

210

experienced. Reactionary depression is normal when we suffer deep grief. Such sadness affects all of our lives, from the emotional to the spiritual, from the cognitive to the physical. Adjusting to the new reality may seem impossible, but it can be done. For many of us this new normal will always be painful and will always be like a hole in the middle of our existence.

Encouragement

The new normal means that things will never be the same. Although the pain gets easier to bear as the scar tissue builds up in our hearts and minds, the pain is always there. No one wants to accept loss. Yet we know we must if we are going to be able to function. You can get to the place of living with this terrible reality. Even when you don't want to go on, you keep putting one foot in front of the other. Sure, some days you don't. Some days you are retreating back into the cave. But eventually you make it out into the light of day more often. You make progress though it may not feel like it.

Moving Forward

1. Pray for God's help as you adjust to things never being the same.

2. Share with a friend, counselor, or pastor how difficult this journey is, how this new normal hurts.

3. Read and reflect on Psalm 91.

Prayer

O Lord, living with this reality is too much to bear. We cannot carry this load. We cannot accept this loss. Give us grace to do what we must. Amen.

42 Grappling with Grief

Jacob was left alone; and a man wrestled with him until daybreak. When the man saw that he did not prevail against Jacob, he struck him on the hip socket; and Jacob's hip was put out of joint as he wrestled with him. Then he said, "Let me go, for the day is breaking." But Jacob said, "I will not let you go, unless you bless me." So he said to him, "What is your name?" And he said, "Jacob." Then the man said, "You shall no longer be called Jacob, but Israel, for you have striven with God and with humans, and have prevailed."
Genesis 32:24-28

Jacob was alone because he had separated his family and flocks into groups and had left them across the river. He was terrified because his brother Esau, who had an army of 400 men, was coming to meet him. He was afraid for his own life and for all his family. The last time he had seen Esau, Jacob had stolen his birthright and his blessing. Esau had been out to kill Jacob. Fear filled Jacob that night.

Jacob wrestled through the night with an opponent, who turned out to be God or an angel of God. So his name was changed from Jacob (Heel Grabber or Trickster) to Israel (Grapples with God). But Jacob's all-night wrestling match left him with a limp. He prevailed but was injured, crippled in the fight. Then he had to face Esau in pain, unable to run and less able to fight. On the other hand, having wrestled with God and prevailed, who was Esau that Jacob should be afraid of him? Grief always leaves us limping, but we are able to go on with the help of God.

Grappling Grief

Night after night
We grapple,
Grief and I.

I wish he would pin me
Get it over with.
Take the win.

Pinning is not his game.
Pain
Punishment
Death
His aim.

The coach yells
From the bench,
"Don't give up!"
"Don't give in!"

"Take my life!"
I want to scream.

But I can't let him
Take me.
"Strive to survive!"
I tell myself.
"Don't let him beat you!"

Another night of
Sweating, swearing
Weeping, crying
Thrashing, turning
Trying to gain advantage.

He squeezes so hard
I can't breathe.
I escape.
But only for a moment.
We lock arms again
And again.

Grief is more agile, more skilled,
Far too experienced
For me,
A champion of thousands of matches
Conquering many a foe.

Who weighed Grief?
Who said we were
In the same weight class?
His muscles are huge,
So much more powerful than I.

How long can I keep this up?
Night after night of wrestling
Exhausted I fall into bed again
Only to be assaulted
By the same opponent.

My face ground into the mat
As he tries to pull me apart
I flip him off me.
He twists back around
Grabbing my leg.
I lock around his waist
Driving with my free leg.

Waking or sleeping
Dreaming or thinking
Relentless grief
Never stops
Never gives up

Night after night
Week after week
Month after month.

Then it happens.
My opponent defaults.
He does not show up
One night.
I almost smile
As I fall asleep.

Midnight
He pounces on me.
He grabs my throat.
I gouge his eyes.
No rules in this match
We go rolling in the
Dirt of night.

Eventually
My assailant does
Miss a night.
Then two.

I limp through my days.
Keep alert in the dark
Grief grips me
Less often.

I begin to sleep
My strained ligaments
My bruised muscles
My broken heart
Begin to heal.

Occasional matches
Still intense
I limp
Hobbling

Exhausted
Enduring.

I manage
To get to my feet
From the mat
No raised hand
In victory,
No applause from
The crowd,
No ribbons
No medal around
My sore neck

I limp off the mat
My trophy
Survival.

I hate it when someone says to me in my grief, "What doesn't kill you, makes you stronger." I can think of lots of exceptions where grief has made a person weaker, even hastened their demise. I've known several couples who, when one died, the other quickly followed.

Yet I do feel I am stronger. Once I got past the first 18 months, I sensed a strength growing in me. Yes, I still feel like I'm missing a limb, like there is a hole in my heart, disabled in some way. At the same time, I am enduring an incredible loss; I have prevailed against grief. We still wrestle from time to time, but I know I will survive. The scars have made me more realistic, more empathetic, more willing to accept what comes, more compassionate.

Encouragement

As grueling as this battle with grief is, you will make it. You will get through this. It is incredibly difficult, but you can survive. You will not be the same. You may become bitter or you may be more accepting of life's tragedies. You may have more compassion for others who suffer. While this war with grief has negatively impacted your life in many ways, too many to count, you may come out a stronger person. You have to become strong just to survive. There is no consolation in that, only the recognition that strength may come as a result of your having wrestled the monster of grief.

Moving Forward

1. Reflect on how you are surviving this grief in spite of the pain.

2. Read and reflect on Psalm 77.

3. What things give you hope? What can you do today to glimpse some light of hope?

4. Listen to a favorite song.

5. Take a walk in a park, in the woods, or at the beach.

Prayer

O Lord, as Jacob wrestled with you through the night, we are wrestling with grief. You know this opponent is too strong for us, too seasoned a warrior. We pray for strength to survive this battle. Help us to endure so that in the end, you will give each of us a new name, congratulating us as one who persists, one who prevails. Amen.

43 A Year Ago Tonight

Do not let your hearts be troubled. Believe in God, believe also in me. In my Father's house there are many dwelling places. If it were not so, would I have told you that I go to prepare a place for you? And if I go and prepare a place for you, I will come again and will take you to myself, so that where I am, there you may be also.
John 14:1-3

This text is one of the most popular to read at Christian funerals. The reason is obvious. Jesus was offering comfort to his disciples. Jesus was preparing his disciples for his own death. He encouraged them to believe that he was going to make ready a place for them. He would return and take them to that place.

When we lose someone we love, we want to cling to the hope that we will be with him or her again. We hang on to this promise that death is not the end, that the Lord will make a place for the one we lost and for us beyond this life. We imagine a blessed reunion with family and friends.

A Year Ago Tonight

It was a year ago tonight
That Rebekah called me
On my cell phone
And blurted out

218

You had been killed
In a motorcycle crash.

I was in a meeting.
When am I not?
I left my piece of fried chicken
Partially eaten on the plate.

I ran out of the United Methodist Men's meeting
Sped home so that I could
Be with Yvonne and Rebekah
Broken hearts all shattered at once.

This year-long grief
Has taught me
How deep a
Grief can go.

Words are
Too weak
To describe the pain.

I miss you more than I can say.
I hope to see you again
On the other side.
I long for that reunion
Where we will no longer be
Father and son
But brothers before the
Father and Son.

See you soon,
My brother,
My son!

I have learned three important things in this year of grief. 1. I can survive a terrible loss with the help of God, family, and friends. 2. People are most important in our lives. 3. God is always with us even in the worst times.

219

Encouragement

It does get easier with time. After six weeks I was not crying myself to sleep every night. I did not wake up with tears in my eyes at the thought of his death every morning as in the beginning. Your grief does not end after a month or a year. Grief goes on, but it changes. The pain is still there but the wounds become more tolerable.

Moving Forward

1. Keep a daily journal, a weekly one, or write your thoughts on the day of the death each month. For example, if he or she died on the 15th of June, then on the 15th of each month jot down your thoughts about anything related to your grief. After a year, read them through to see the changes in your thoughts.

2. On the anniversary of your loved one's death, take time to be with those closest to her or him. My wife, daughter, and I took the day off just to be together on the first anniversary and plan to continue that tradition.

3. Read and reflect on John 14:1-7.

Prayer

Lord, you give us the promise of eternal life. We latch on to that promise and hold on for dear life. Help us to believe as Jesus encouraged his friends to believe. May this promise help us endure the dark days of grief. Amen.

COMFORTING EACH OTHER

44 The Breath of God

In the beginning when God created the heavens and the earth, the earth
was a formless void and darkness covered the face of the deep, while a
wind from God swept over the face of the waters.
Genesis 1:1-2

The Bible begins with the sentence above. God's wind or spirit
(same word in Hebrew) moves on the watery chaos to create the
world. When death comes, the wind stops.

Becalmed

The wind has died.
My soul becalmed.
Dead in the water.
No breeze or balm.

We are making
Good time
On a beam reach
The sun glistening off the water
The salty spray lightly showering us
The boat gliding through the glass.

221

A family of dolphins laugh
Jumping alongside
Our little boat
As we move gladly through time.

The days we got to sail
Together were too few
But the best of
Father and son.

The storm comes up suddenly
No warning of this front
Moving in on us
Lightning, thunder
Black clouds
Raining down so hard
We cannot not see
In front of our boat.

Take down the sails!
Main and jib.
The rain so cold we are shivering.
Would lightning strike the mast?

Now he is gone
Washed away
In the memory of a storm
Shared together.

The sun beats down on me,
Not a cloud in the sky
No wind
No slicing through the water
No gurgling under the hull
No mate to take the tiller
No son to learn the ropes

The sails hang lifeless

Mourning his absence
The silence is overwhelming
The wind refuses to blow
Or even to whisper.

The lines begin to clang
Against the metal mast
Tolling the news of his death
As the boat rocks
In the sickening swells.

Is it out of respect for
My sailor son
Or out of cruelty
That there is
No breath of wind?

God formed the man
From the dust of the ground
And blew in his nostrils
The breath of life.
So the story goes
Of life on land.

What happens
When the breath is gone
And the wind dies
Out on the water?
I am left gasping for meaning
Longing for purpose
Waiting to move forward
Wondering
Will the wind ever return?

What if the wind
Were to return?
Would it matter?

Where will I wander

On this landless sea?
Is there no destination,
Just destiny?
No paradise to ponder?

What need is there to navigate?
There is no chart,
No course to plot
That will take me to him.

The glare off the water
Reflects the reality
That I am now alone;
Imprisoned, confined
To a solitary fiberglass cell.

Like driftwood floating
On fathoms of despair
Like dust scattered
On the surface of the water
My soul lies lifeless
Waiting for
The breath
Of God.

When our son died, I felt I had been punched in the gut. The wind was knocked out of me. When that happens physically, it only lasts a few moments until you can breathe again. But emotionally, that feeling can last for weeks, months (will it be years?). Actual physical fatigue has been much more a part of my grief than I ever would have imagined. I have been worn out physically. Sleep has been difficult. Both mind and body have been numb from despair. I rushed back into my work not knowing what else to do. While it distracted me a little from my grief, working added to the fatigue. I have learned that others really want to help and that I should let them.

Encouragement

The physical and emotional weight of grief can be devastating. Do what you need to do to take care of yourself—even if it's frowned on by others. Take as much time off as you can. Stay close to family and friends. When people offer to cook for you or do other tasks to ease your burden, don't be Stoic. Take them up on these offers if it is a help to you. Life has been cruel to you. Be kind to yourself so you can begin to heal. It's not being selfish. It's survival.

Moving Forward

1. Make a list of practical things people can do for you—from making phone calls to mowing your lawn. Make a list of items people can purchase for you when they are shopping, saving you trips when it's difficult to face the public. Be ready to share these lists with others, when friends offer.

2. Read and reflect on Psalm 104.

Prayer

God of the wind, may the gentle breeze of your presence, fill our lives. May your breath renew the life within us as we struggle with grief and despair. Help us, O Lord. Amen.

45 Healing the Broken

My joy is gone, grief is upon me,
my heart is sick.
Hark, the cry of my poor people
from far and wide in the land:
"Is the LORD not in Zion?
Is her King not in her?"
Jeremiah 8:18-19b

For the hurt of my poor people I am hurt,
I mourn, and dismay has taken hold of me.
Is there no balm in Gilead?
Is there no physician there?
Why then has the health of my poor people
not been restored?
Jeremiah 8:21-22

The prophet Jeremiah warned his people of the impending doom, that their land would be conquered by the Babylonians unless they repented. They did not listen.

In the ancient way of thinking, Jeremiah was a traitor because once a prophet releases the word of the Lord, he (or she) takes part in making it happen. So this prophet actually set in motion the destruction of his own country. The king even imprisoned Jeremiah.

Still Jeremiah loved his own people. He walked with them through the capture of Jerusalem. He was there for the destruction. He wanted to bring healing to them, both before the destruction and afterward. He felt powerless to make a positive difference. As we watch others grieve, we often feel powerless to bring comfort to them.

A Broken Crutch

"How do you mend
A broken heart?"
I hear the crooner sing
Of his own.

How do you heal
Another's pain?
How do I soothe
His mother's loss?

How do I make it
Easier for his sister?
What can I do to
Calm the heaving
Sobs of his grandparents?

Is there no balm in Gilead?
Is there no solace that I can offer?
Is there nothing I can do
To make it better?

No trite phrase can
Help with the pain.
Flowers and cards--
Nice, but not healing.

Only one salve
I have found
To temporarily cool
The burning heartache.

227

Only one source of
Light to shine
In the dark night
Of their souls.

It is a flickering
Fire that only
Offers intermittent
Flashes of ease.

The cost to me
Seems exorbitant.
Hardly worth the price
I pay for ephemeral
Relief for them.

What is it?
Crushed love.

To be broken
Before them,
To be broken
With them,
To be shattered
By the same grief
That has crushed them.
To limp alongside
The lame in spirit.

To suffer
With them
With Him.

Don't toss aside
The broken crutch.
Don't retreat into
Your own grief.

Allow them to lean
On you
Even if the burden
Splinters your heart.

Risk them knowing
How broken
You are.

The puzzle of grief is never finished until we bring the pieces of our broken hearts together. I found that being vulnerable with my own pain, and sharing it with those close to me, moved all of us toward healing. As a male I saw myself as a problem solver. I had to be the strong one, the rock. I had to have the answers. As a pastor, I help people heal.

It was not until I admitted being wounded that I felt myself begin to heal. When I owned my loss and my devastation by sharing it with my family and friends, I began to feel a little relief. Confessing my brokenness actually helped bring healing to others. So now I see myself more as a wounded healer, who helps others most by limping alongside them.

Encouragement

Grief may be the most difficult for those who want to take care of others, for those who want to appear strong, and for those who don't want to admit weakness. I was all of those. Perhaps you struggle with all of those issues. I admit it still makes no sense to me that the most helpful I can be to others is to be open with them about my own pain.

If you want to help yourself and those around you who are grieving, don't close yourself off to them. Cry with them. Listen to them. Be willing to share your pain with them. This is not easy for many of us. Yet it will help you and those who share your loss in this grief process.

Moving Forward

1. Set up an appointment with another person who shares your grief, for the sole purpose of listening to each other's stories of pain—even if you think you already know.

2. Write a letter to God telling how much you are hurting.

3. Read the passion of Christ (Mark 14:17-15:39). Reflect on how Jesus as a human being must have felt. Relate that to your grief.

4. Read the lyrics, sing, or listen to the song "There Is a Balm In Gilead."

Prayer
Lord, you called us to weep with those who weep. We know that's what you do. May we sense your presence as you come alongside us, crying tears of grief with us. Thank you for your love, O God. Amen.

46 Being There

Now when Job's three friends heard of all these troubles that had come upon him, each of them set out from his home – Eliphaz the Temanite, Bildad the Shuhite, and Zophar the Naamathite. They met together to go and console and comfort him. When they saw him from a distance, they did not recognize him, and they raised their voices and wept aloud; they tore their robes and threw dust in the air upon their heads. They sat with him on the ground seven days and seven nights, and no one spoke a word to him, for they saw that his suffering was very great.
Job 2:11-13

Job's friends, Eliphaz, Bildad, and Zophar, Job's comforters, as we sometimes call them, often get a bad rap. Yes, later in the story they did say things that would have been better left unsaid. They chastised Job for not confessing his sins, not admitting that the tragedies that had befallen him were his fault. They argued with him about why he had lost so much.

Note, however, that his friends started out on the right track. They identified with his tragedy. Tearing one's clothing and putting dust on one's head were signs of mourning in the ancient Near East. They wept aloud for their friend and for the difficulty Job had endured. The most important thing they did was to sit with him for seven days in silence.

The most meaningful way we comfort one another is by being there for each other. The silent presence of someone who loves

231

you in the midst of your pain is a great gift. Yes, sometimes we want to be alone in our grief. True friends will respect that. Job's friends were true comforters in the beginning.

Being There for Our Family

Not even
In our worst
Nightmares
Had we imagined
Such pain on
The death of our son,
Our daughter's brother.

Nothing could
Make it better
Or make it
Go away.

But never
In our dreams
Did we anticipate
Or deserve
Such friends
Who were with us.

Eating, driving,
Laughing, talking,
Crying, giving
Listening, sharing,
Being there
With us.

That's what
Got us through,
Still does.

People wanted to comfort us. Not everyone was good at it. Some were obviously uncomfortable. It should not have been a revelation to me that some people are not good at offering comfort. My wife and I have spent a lifetime being there for people. We both have the gift of compassion. Many people do not. They are good at other things, but not walking with you in your grief. I had to move past not being helped by some because of their lack of empathy. I am coming to accept that we all have different gifts. They meant well.

After a week of respectful silence, Job's friends tried to straighten out his theology and attempted to get him to confess his wrongdoings. It was obvious to them that God was punishing him for sin, of which he needed to repent. In the end their visit was really about them and their agenda, not about Job and his pain. I had to forgive my friends who were too much like Job's comforters in the later chapters of the book.

Encouragement

Not everyone is good at comforting others. Not everyone knows how to be there for you in your grief. You may be disappointed in some of your friends for not being present in your crisis. Cut them some slack because most of us don't know how to help someone who is grieving.

I hope you have friends who are there for you. Do not hesitate to lean on them. If they are true friends, they will be grateful for your willingness to let them help. No one can make the pain subside. However, it does help if someone will sit on the ground with you in silence at this low point in your life.

Moving Forward

1. If you have someone who has been there for you, thank them. Write a note. Tell them how much their presence has meant to you.

2. When you are able, offer your presence to a friend who is hurting.

3. Read and reflect on Psalm 62.

Prayer

Lord, you have called us to love one another. You have shown us love beyond our comprehension. Enable us to love. May we be there for others as you have been for us. Amen.

47 A Lotus Flower

David therefore pleaded with God for the child; David fasted, and went in and lay all night on the ground. The elders of his house stood beside him, urging him to rise from the ground; but he would not, nor did he eat food with them. On the seventh day the child died.
2 Samuel 12:16-18a

Months into her pregnancy the obstetrician says there is no heartbeat. They go to the hospital where she endures the process of giving birth to a stillborn child. Other parents are shocked when they expect a living child but the child dies during the birth. Many women have suffered the heartache of a miscarriage. Losing a baby crushes the hope and joyful anticipation that fill the hearts of parents-to-be as well as their family and friends.

When I visit parents whose babies have died at our local hospital, there is a lotus flower taped to their doors in the neonatal unit. The lotus flower alerts the medical staff that the mother inside that room has lost her baby. They need to know before they open the door so they can distinguish tears of indescribable joy from tears of utter sorrow. They can be ready to be compassionate and caring for those who grieve. As a parent who lost a grown child, I can only imagine the pain of those parents.

A Father's Hope

Instead of cuddling her
In my arms
To show her to family
And friends,
I carry her in
A little white casket,
A coffin, her first cradle.

Instead of passing her around
From aunt to grandmother
From grandfather to uncle,
Each places a rose
On the lid of the casket
Already resting in this
Shallow grave.

No coos or giggles
No baby talk
But quiet sobs
Silent tears

How unfair
To rob her
Of life
Before she breathed
That first breath!

What had she done to
Offend you, Almighty God?!
Was her wiggling
In her mother's womb
Displeasing to you?

Back at the house
I turn off the light in
Her nursery,
Shut the door,

Lock it.

I won't go there.
No one allowed in.
Her welcoming space,
Nurturing place.

I wish I could close off
This space in my heart
Reserved for her alone.
Once filled with light,
Love and hope.
Now dark with despair
Walls closing in
Crushing me.

My heart nursery
Was already filled,
Decorated with dreams
Of loving smiles
As she looked up
Into my face,
Of joy and laughter;
Of holding her hand
As she took her first steps;
Of teaching her to ride
A bike;
Furnished with imaginings of
Walking her to kindergarten,
Eventually down the aisle,
Of a child that looked
Just like her.

Hope is long,
Filled with wonderful
Anticipations.

What hope is there now?
Jesus said, "I go to prepare a place . . ."

Is her nursery with you, Lord?

As she opens her eyes
For the first time,
Does she look into
The loving face of her Father
And mine?

Can hope go that far?
Forgive my envy
That you get to hold her,
To love on her,
To know her.

Will there be a rocker
Next to yours
So that one day
I can have a turn?

Now she is yours
Though I would not have
Given her up for adoption
Not even to you, Lord.

Call me selfish or greedy
But I wanted to be her daddy
And for her to be my
Little girl.

That was my hope.

I put my hope in you,
O God, that
One day she will
Call me, "Daddy"
Too.

As I walk with friends who suffer grief, my heart breaks for them. Because of my own grief, I understand their pain at a level

238

that I probably would not have, had I not suffered such loss. It tears off the scabs where my heart has partially healed. Even though their grief is different, I bleed with them. As difficult as it is for me, I make sure I am there for them, as others have been there for me.

Encouragement

Unfortunately losing of a baby is too common, either through stillbirth or miscarriage. In times past that loss was kept quiet. I only learned decades after she was a grandmother that my mother had lost a baby. It was my sister who told me. I have never discussed that loss with my mother. My mother-in-law also lost a baby. But they never spoke of their losses.

Losing a baby is such a hard loss for many reasons. Hope and joy are turned into bitter sadness. Dreams turn into a nightmare. All those who had been anticipating the celebration now join in grief. Baby showers must be cancelled. If you already had a baby shower, guilt over having taken those gifts for nothing piles on the guilt you already feel. You blame yourself for the baby's death even though you are not to blame. Hang on to those around you, who are supportive during this difficult time.

Moving Forward

1. Join a support group for grieving parents.

2. Make a memory box with items related to your child who did not get to experience life outside the womb, or whose life was cut short. (Sometimes hospitals will help with this.)

3. Read and reflect on being consoled and consoling others in 2 Corinthians 1:1-7.

Prayer

Lord, our hopes were dashed to the ground. Dreadful sorrow has pushed aside our hopeful anticipation. Our hearts once filled with love and longing are empty and broken. Bring healing to our lives. Carry us through these dark days. Help us to be there for others. Amen.

GOD AND GRIEF

48 Good Friday

When they came to the place that is called The Skull, they crucified Jesus there with the criminals, one on his right and one on his left.
Luke 23:33

On Good Friday every year our church offers a three-hour service at noon. We invite seven local ministers or priests to preach on each of the seven last words of Jesus from the cross. I know it's traditional to have a three-hour service on Good Friday. However, when I came to this congregation in 2009, I hated having such a long service focused on the suffering and death of Jesus. I had been involved in effective Good Friday services that were only an hour or an hour and a half. But it was the tradition in this congregation so I accepted it. I told myself, "After all, if Christ suffered on a cross for me, it is a tiny thing for me to endure a three-hour service centered around his suffering." Then my son died.

Good Friday Condolences

"My condolences" seems so weak
A thing to say
To One who lost so much.

240

I am sorry, God,
For the death of Jesus
Your Son.

I am sorry for the Romans who put him to death,
For the Jews who misunderstood him,
For the Christians who misrepresent him,
For all us humans whose sin
His death atones.

That I should even speak to you
About his death
Seems offensive.

But now that I have lost a son,
My heart is broken,
In my infinitesimally small way
I offer my condolences.

Not that I can understand
Who you are
Or what you lost.

Yet I offer my sorrow,
My sacrifice,
A broken heart.

Please accept
These condolences
From a father
Who has also
Lost his
Only son.

I've learned that as I was able to hang on to my faith, my understanding of God changed. At first I felt guilty for seeing God through the lens of anger and bitterness. Then on the first Good Friday after my son died, I began to see God through the darkness of sorrow. My view of God has been changing since the loss of my son.

At first that was disturbing. After all, my livelihood comes from how I see and interpret God to the people in my congregation. It was unsettling to think that my theology was in such transition. I am not saying that I had God completely figured out before this loss. What I mean is that I was comfortable with my theology that had grown gently over the years.

The loss of Samuel, Jr. shattered my understanding of God. Picking up the pieces and figuring out what new collage of God I could assemble in my mind has been part of my grieving. Being faithful to God and being honest with my pain have together created turmoil for my brain to make sense of it all. Yet one of the gains has been to re-claim the idea of a God who suffers. Many Christians talk about Jesus who suffered and died on a cross. But what about a grieving Father who had to watch his Son be tortured? Somehow it has been helpful to think of God as a grieving parent.

Encouragement

If you can hang on to your faith, it will probably be different. That's okay. You may feel your faith strengthened after your loss. Many people do eventually become stronger spiritually in spite of their loss. However, you may walk away from faith entirely. You may quit believing in God altogether. You may leave the church. I understand that.

Even as a pastor, I have certainly had those thoughts and know walking away was a possibility for me. Let me encourage you. Whether your loss has strengthened your belief in God or has completely dismantled it, God understands. It's okay. God loves us whether or not we love God back. God believes in us whether or not we believe in God.

Moving Forward

1. Read and reflect on Jeremiah 20:7-12. (Jeremiah accuses God of bullying him into his prophetic role, which has not turned out well.)

2. Read, sing or listen to "The Old Rugged Cross," by George Bennard.

Prayer

Lord, sometimes we believe in you, appreciate you and offer our praises to you. Other times we are angry with you, accuse you, and walk away from you. Help us as we battle grief to come to grips with our faith in you. May we grow in our understanding of your love and grace even through the misery of grief. Amen.

49 "God Doesn't Care About That!"

Love never ends. But as for prophecies, they will come to an end; as for tongues, they will cease; as for knowledge, it will come to an end. For we know only in part, and we prophesy only in part; but when the complete comes, the partial will come to an end. When I was a child, I spoke like a child, I thought like a child, I reasoned like a child; when I became an adult, I put an end to childish ways. For now we see in a mirror, dimly, but then we will see face to face. Now I know only in part; then I will know fully, even as I have been fully known. And now faith, hope, and love abide, these three; and the greatest of these is love.
1 Corinthians 13:8-13

The secretary at the funeral home that was going to cremate our son's body had decided that she would handle our son's case rather than handing it over to a funeral director. Big mistake.

She learned from an answering machine message that I was a pastor. I don't normally let people know what I do, because people act differently when they know you are clergy. Some treat you like a newly found best buddy who believes just like they do even though they don't know what you think. Invariably they start preaching an impromptu sermon or start bragging on their pastor, neither of which is welcome.

Other people don't know how to deal with you. It's awkward. Some automatically assume you are narrow-minded, uneducated, and would probably burn a Quran given the opportunity. They treat you with mild disdain at best. When the secretary called back, we had the following conversation.

The Conversation

She said,
"That's wonderful
You are a pastor.
I'm a Christian, too."

"Was your son
A believer?"

Silence
Stuttering
Stammering

I finally said, "I don't think
That's an appropriate
Question."

"He believed in Jesus.
You know he is
With the Lord, right?"

I managed to mutter,
"I'm not sure
He even believed in God."

Without listening
In her zeal she pressed,
"Well you know he's
With God in eternity, right?"

Again I said,
"It's inappropriate for
You to ask that question."

Not hearing me

She said, "I guess
You'll have to wait
To find out when
You get there."

Then she began
Talking about her
Grown children
Who were all
Still alive.
All saved.

As a pastor and father who was struggling with my son's sudden death, the last thing I needed to be questioned about was my son's eternal destiny. The secretary's intention may have been to comfort me. But of course, it had the opposite effect. I repeated to her that it was an inappropriate question, but she did not seem to listen or understand what I was saying. I was hurt and horrified at such a cavalier attitude.

I was sharing this disturbing experience with a friend who earned a Master of Divinity degree before I did. I questioned out loud, "I don't know if my son had faith in God. I can't say that he was a believer. He had been an atheist at one point."

My friend put his arm around me and said, "My God doesn't care about that." It was at once both the kindest word of pastoral care and the most profound theological statement anyone had ever said to me. I'm still trying to get my mind around the thought that God may not judge us by our theological positions but by more profound issues of life and work, that God may see beyond my puny faith and my son's apparent lack of faith. Perhaps God is more like Jesus and does not condemn us at all for not being part of religious institutions. I continue to be comforted by that kind remark motivated by my friend's love for me in a time of deep grief.

Encouragement

Some people think they have this life and the afterlife all figured out. Perhaps you are in that theological camp. If your assurance brings you comfort, I encourage you to hang on to it. If,

246

on the other hand, you are unsure or unclear about what happens when we die, then join the vast majority of us. None of us knows as much as we think we know about God or others. Sorrow teaches us that.

I am reminded of the story from India of the five blind men who were asked to tell what the elephant is like. One, who was touching the trunk, said, "The elephant is like a big snake." The second, who was touching the tail, said, "No the elephant is like a rope." The third said, "You are both wrong." As he felt the elephant's side, he said, "The elephant is like a wall." The fourth disagreed, and said, "The elephant is like a tree," as he felt the leg of the elephant. Finally, the fifth man, who was grasping the elephant's ear, said, "No, the elephant is like a giant leaf moving back and forth in the wind."

As Saint Paul suggests in the above passage, we now know only in part; God is much bigger than any of us can grasp. God's love for us and for those we care about is beyond comprehension and extends into eternity.

Moving Forward

1. Write down those things that you know to be true about God, which bring comfort to you.

2. Make a list of the statements that people have said to you in your time of grief that have been helpful to you.

3. Read and reflect on 1 Corinthians 13:9-13.

Prayer

O Lord, we admit we do not know you completely. You have revealed yourself in Jesus Christ to be a God who cares about tiny sparrows, a God who cares so much about us, you have numbered the hairs of our heads. Help us to bask in the rays of your love that break through the darkness of our grief. As we trudge along beneath the angry clouds of grief, strengthen our faith in the eternal light of your gentle love that shines above what we can see and what we can know. Amen.

50 "God Won't Give You More than You Can Handle"

"Is there anyone among you who, if your child asks for bread, will give a stone? Or if the child asks for a fish, will give a snake? If you then, who are evil, know how to give good gifts to your children, how much more will your Father in heaven give good things to those who ask him!"
Matthew 7:9-11

Isn't Jesus saying that God gives us good things? When we say, "God won't give you more than you can handle," are we saying that the loss or tragedy someone is experiencing is a gift from God? How can we suggest that a God of love would cause such things as cancer, AIDS, and heart disease?

My friend said to me, "God won't give you any more than you can handle." He meant to encourage me in the loss of my son. I did not respond. Yet inside I cried at his cruel thought. "Are you saying that God gave my son's death to me, like a gift? So, not only do I have to endure this loss, but I have to believe in a God who would be that cruel to me. You want me to believe in a God like that?" I walked away.

God Won't Give

So this is a gift?
This death I have felt,

248

This loss
I endure.

Shouldn't I be
Able to refuse
A gift?
To walk away
From Pandora's box?

No loving God
Would give such
Heartache to a child.

If human,
We'd lock up
The child abuser.
He wouldn't survive
A month in prison.

The other inmates
Would make certain
Justice was done,
Yard justice.

So we worship
A God who tortures
Those he created
In his image?
He abuses his followers,
Inflicts pain on his friends?

Can we actually
Believe in such a deity?

Can we blame God
For Auschwitz, for Dachau
Hiroshima, Pearl Harbor?

Can we lay on God

The guilt of
Bloodthirsty tyrants
Abusive parents
Cruel spouses
Murderers
Rapists?

Such thinking
Corrupts our hope
Destroys our faith
Mocks the divine Shepherd.

We turn
Unchangeable Goodness
Into
Diabolical sadism.

My God gives no
Such gifts,
Inflicts no pain,
Tortures no one.

My God was
Tortured for us,
Bore the pain,
Bled for our sins.

My God does not
Swing clubs
Smashing skulls.

My God does not
Squeeze us to death
With congenital
Heart failure
Or slowly take over
Healthy cells with
Cancerous invaders.
Or cover the brain

With plaque to rob
Us of who we are.

My God is the great physician
Who heals,
The social worker
Who protects,
The big brother
Who steps between
To take the blows,
The mother
Who nurses
The father who carries
His little boy.

This Christian cliché is often spoken with the intention of encouraging another person. I've probably said, "God won't give you more than you can handle," meaning that God will help you through this. It would be better simply to say, "God will help you" instead of ascribing some tortuous act to God.

When my friend said this to me, I realized he was saying that I should be able to handle this loss. Since I did not think I was handling it well, I felt even worse about myself as a Christian. His attempt at encouraging me actually inflicted more discomfort.

I am still learning to accept the intention of comfort from others even if the words are offensive. As Christians we need to re-think many of the things we say to people when they are grieving. Words matter just as much as intention.

Encouragement

One of the annoying and frustrating aspects of the process of grief is hearing this and other Christian clichés, which can truly be offensive. Such comments often feel like someone is kicking you after you've fallen down. You may react by questioning the person for disseminating such nonchalant theology. That is certainly appropriate. However, most people have not thought about these sayings, they just repeat them because they come to mind.

251

You can choose to look past the words unless it's a good friend who is willing to change in order to help you and others. In that case you might respond by asking what they are saying about God when they say, "God won't give you more than you can handle." Did God cause this accident, inflict this disease, or motivate the murderer?

If you are offended, you can say so. Or you can ignore the words and give them the benefit of the doubt. I'm not sure there is a good way to respond to such a thoughtless saying, so I would encourage you to do what works for you. I wish I could give you a formula so you could let such insensitive statements roll off of you like water off a duck's back. I don't think one exists, especially as you go through the pain of grief. I would hope that you would not allow this statement to lead you to give up on God, who loves you and is walking with you in this process.

Don't allow this statement to discourage you by suggesting something is wrong with you as you are struggling with loss. Loss cannot be handled like taking care of a flat tire or a problem at the office. In fact, grief handles us.

Moving Forward
1. Read Psalm 42. Reflect on the idea that God helps us in our time of grief.

2. Draw a mental (or actual) picture of how you see God in your grief—good or bad. How does that make you feel? Share these feelings and thoughts with a trusted friend.

Prayer
Thank you, Lord, for offering goodness and comfort to us. Through Jesus Christ, you have revealed yourself as kind, compassionate, patient, loving, and merciful. You are a God who heals, not a God who hurts. Help us choose our words wisely as we offer comfort to one another. May we forgive others who hurt us as you have forgiven us. Amen.

51 God Laments

Then Jesus gave a loud cry and breathed his last. And the curtain of the temple was torn in two, from top to bottom.
Mark 15:37-38

At the death of Jesus the temple curtain was torn top down. What does that mean? Christian theologians have long pointed to God granting access to the holy of holies, the place where only the high priest was allowed once a year on the Day of Atonement. We have been taught that because of the atoning, sacrificial death of Jesus Christ, now all have direct access to God. God has opened his presence to everyone.

Grief reveals another perspective. "Then Jacob tore his garments, and put sackcloth on his loins, and mourned for his son many days." (Genesis 37:34)

In the ancient world when a loved one died, a person's first reaction was to tear his/her clothing. Clothing was handmade and very expensive. This act of tearing one's clothing communicated that one's very heart had been ripped open by the loss. This act of anguish symbolized physical pain at the death of a loved one.

The Torn Robe

The heavy curtain
Three stories high

253

Interwoven threads of
Blue, purple, crimson
Fine twisted white linen
The lovely robe
That hid your presence
From us.

You tore open
Your robe
In anger and anguish
A Father's love
Exposed
At the bloody death of
Your son.

Your soft refined garment
Worn in holiness and dignity
In beauty and elegance
Cherubim dancing across
The rich panels of human cloth.

Death desecrates
Death devastates
Exposing a brokenness
At the heart
Of holiness.

Fashion flung aside
Dignity tossed away
Holiness abandoned
Heartache revealed

A God of emotions?
Of feelings?
Of grief?

You sobbed;
The earth quaked.
You closed your eyes

254

In pain;
Darkness covered the earth.
You grabbed your robe
Tearing it from top to bottom.

The ark of the covenant
The mercy seat
Statues of cherubim
Relics all gone
From this most holy place

Your ancient voice
Garbled from behind
The layered curtain
Thundered commands
And reprimands.

You tore your robe
Allowing us to see
Our God
Whimpering in grief
Trembling at loss
Weeping with me.

Revealing the heart
Of holiness
Not logic, But love.
Not spotless,
But tear-stained
And dirty.
Not mountain high
But gutter low.
Not restricted and elite
But grimy and calloused.

Holy of holies
Not separate from,
But deeper in,
Than we ever imagined.

God got out
God escaped
From his holy prison
The catalyst?
The death of his Son.

The secret is out
God is love,
Love that cannot be contained
Or controlled
Wild love
That rends garments
Endures heartache and loss
With us and for us.

The idea of a God who suffers with us, who weeps when we weep, who mourns with us, is profoundly helpful to me and to many. Instead of a God far removed from us, high and lifted up, transcendent and unreachable, I see a God of love who lets go of all his grandeur to walk with us lowly mourners of planet earth. It means for me that God is present and real as I walk in this pain.

Encouragement

I hope it is helpful for you to think that in your pain, God is not the one who afflicts you, but the one who comforts you. Rather than seeing a God who judges you and finds you guilty, think of a God who is on your side, your defense attorney. God does not condemn you but consoles you. Grief twists our ideas of God in our dark emotions and pain. It's hard to picture God as loving and kind in our loss. Yet, the New Testament reveals just such a God. I pray that this idea of God and that God's very presence will comfort you.

Moving Forward

1. Write a poem or song about God's love for you in the midst of pain.

2. Write a thank you card to God for being there for you in this terrible time.

256

3. Hold on to a cross or crucifix and meditate on the fact that Christ died for you and for your loved one.

4. Read and reflect on Psalm 34, particularly verse 18.

Prayer
Lord, we thank you for loving us in our pain. Thank you for being with us in our grief. We are grateful to you, O God, for coming down to us as we stumble through this heartache. Please continue to walk with us and carry us when we cannot walk. Amen.

52 Take This Cup from Me

They went to a place called Gethsemane; and he said to his disciples, "Sit here while I pray." He took with him Peter and James and John, and began to be distressed and agitated. And said to them, "I am deeply grieved, even to death; remain here, and keep awake." And going a little farther, he threw himself on the ground and prayed that, if it were possible, the hour might pass from him. He said, "Abba, Father, for you all things are possible; remove this cup from me; yet, not what I want, but what you want."
Mark 14:32-36

Jesus prayed to escape the suffering that lay before him. None of us wants to suffer. We certainly do not want those whom we love to experience pain. Perhaps the greatest suffering in life is the pain of grief over the death of someone we loved.

Take This Cup From Me

Jesus prayed,
If it be possible,
Take this cup from me
The cup of suffering and death
He was about to endure
Because he surrendered to your will
That your own son be tortured and killed.

258

O, that it would be possible
For you to turn back the
Hands of time
Before his crash.
If you could rewrite history
For him
For me.

If I could have
Chosen to suffer
And die
Instead of my son,
I would have asked
To drink from that cup.
I would have demanded
To become drunk
With my own blood
To have endured
Whatever pain
To spare him.

But the cup of his death
Is too bitter to force
Down my throat.
Like acid eating through
My esophagus and
The rest of my body
Melting me into
A mournful mass.

This cup is too much
For me.
Take this cup from me!

Would you
If you could?

Would you have removed

The bitter cup from Jesus
If you could have?

We assume your
Benevolence,
Theologize
That this was the only way
To save us sinners--
For him to suffer
And die.

So what kind of Father
Are you?
What kind of God
Could not have written
A different world story
So that your Son
Would have been spared?

Would that there was
A divine council or
A celestial
"Department of Children
And Families"
To report
That you abandoned
Your son!

I would not have
Abandoned mine.

Are you not guilty
Of child abuse?
Or at least extreme
Neglect
As your son cried out
To you
"My God, My God
why have you

forsaken me?"

Jesus had declared,
"I and my Father
are One!"
Did you not buy in?
Did you bow out
Of your familial
Obligation?

Like a deadbeat dad,
An absentee father?

Am I wrong to think
So little of you?
Were you there?
Were you really
One all along?
Did you remain
The loving Father
Jesus always talked about
Until the end?

Forgive me, Lord.
I was blind.
I did not see it until now.
Your love goes beyond
What I ever imagined.

This cup that I refuse to drink
The cup of my son's death
Is one that you accepted
Willing to own
The brokenness
Of a grieving parent.

You stood there
By Mary
Watching your own son

As they nailed him
To the cross.

Every blow of the
Hammer drove deep
Into your heart.
Your pain must have been
Even greater than
His mother's.

You were a
Loving dad
Desperate to do anything
To save your son
Restrained only
By the choice
That you had made
To drink from that cup
For the sake of humanity
For my sake, too.

You knew full well
Your pain
Would be
Worse than his.

You were not an
Angry Father who
Crucified his Son
For the sake of righteousness.
But a Dad
Who was
Crucified
With Him
For the sake of love.

In your anguish
You ripped open your robe
The temple curtain

Torn in two
From top to bottom

Then your broken heart
Could no longer
Stand to be
Without him
So you raised him
From the dead!

Dad, the divine
Echoed the words
Of his own son
For all the universe to hear
"Take this cup
From me!"

With that you raised him
From the dead
Alive again
Father and Son
Reunited.

You broke the rules
Of life and death because
Your love could not
Keep you from him.

Then you rolled the stone
From the tomb to show
Us all what the love
Of our Father had done.

Easter gives me hope
That you will take this
Cup from me,
That I will see my son
Alive again.

The loss of my son has been extremely painful for me. I hate the suffering and sadness that has come into my life. Like Jesus praying in the Garden of Gethsemane, I found myself praying for God to remove this pain. I have not been as committed as Jesus to the will of God. I have not prayed, "but your will be done." I do not want to accept the reality of his death. Feelings of sadness, pain, anger, guilt, and confusion all mix to make the experience of grief the worst kind of suffering. I am learning that as Jesus accepted the arrest, torture and death that was to come, I have to accept this suffering of grief.

Encouragement

If you could, you would change what happened. None of us wants to accept the death of a loved one. We want God to make it go away, to reverse the events that led up to their death. Unfortunately, we have to go through the suffering to come to acceptance. Beginning with denial, we resist such a journey. Many of us feel we have been dragged kicking and screaming down into this valley of the shadow of death. Yet we have to go through many dark nights and difficult days before we can come to a place of peace and light.

Moving Forward

1. Write down all your reasons why your loved one should not have died.

2. Express to God how the death of your loved one has impacted you and why it should not have happened. (God is not offended by raised voices and angry words. God understands.)

3. Gaze on a cross or crucifix and reflect on the heartache of God the Father.

4. Focus on a butterfly and reflect on the love motivating the resurrection of Jesus.

5. Read, sing or listen to the hymn, "Rock of Ages, Cleft for Me," by Augustus M. Toplady.

Prayer

Lord, you have revealed yourself as a suffering God, an idea which boggles our minds. Help us to relate to you in our suffering. Walk with us in our pain. Carry us through this storm by your loving presence with us. Amen.

WHAT HAPPENS WHEN WE DIE?

53 Waiting for Me to Come Home

"Out of the window she peered,
the mother of Sisera gazed through the lattice:
'Why is his chariot so long in coming?
Why tarry the hoofbeats of his chariots?'
Judges 5:28

This ancient poem imagined what the mother of the slain Canaanite general Sisera must have been thinking when he did not return from war. She had not received the news that her warrior son was dead. The author anticipated the grief she would endure when she learned he would never be coming home again.

Waiting for Daddy

"Daddy?" He asked
When he heard
The mail carrier
Dropping off letters.
"Daddy home?"

"No. Not yet,"
His mother replied.

Before he could
Form a sentence
He longed for my return
From many hours at work.

"Daddy," his first word
His first longing
My absence
His pain.

As soon as I walk
In the door
He latches onto
My leg.

I continue walking
With him attached,
"Where is my son?
Where is Samuel?"

Giggling, "Here,"
Not letting go of his grip.
I pry him off
Scoop him up
In my arms.

He's superman
Flying through the sky.
We wrestle on the floor
Play with matchbox cars
Stuffed animals.

Always too soon
I have to leave
The adventure.

Now our roles reversed
I ache to see you.

Your absence
My pain.

I long to see you
Come through the door,
To hear your laugh.

Were it only a country
Or an ocean
That separated us
A plane ride
A few days travel,
I would be with you.

Death is the divider
That tears us apart
Shatters the family
Breaks the heart.

My aching soul
Longs to hug you
To know you are safe
To be with you
To carry you
In my arms again.

I had promised
We would come to California
To see you
Tickets purchased
Motel rooms booked
For our grand adventure.

You were so excited
You could not sleep.

You were not
At your Lancaster house
To welcome us

When we arrived.

We stayed there as
You had requested
Sleeping on air mattresses
Breathing the cool
Desert night air.

At the funeral home
They handed you to me,
A colorful cylindrical
Cardboard container
With your ashes inside.

So I carried you again
But only your ashes
To the car
Back to your home.

No longer
Your house
No more your place.
You've abandoned
Time, home, and space.

Are you waiting
In that home
Jesus promised?

Do you long to see me?
Are you asking, "Is it my Dad?"
Every time the door opens?
Are you anticipating my arrival?

Do I get to come
Home?

We all have regrets. Death shines a spotlight on what we wish
we had done or not done. I regret that I did not spend more time

with my children as they were growing up. I wish I had visited with my son more as an adult. Death has taught me again it's the people that matter. What is important in life becomes painfully apparent when life ends and opportunities vanish. We cannot go back. We must exist in the empty present with hope of a future that will banish our loss by re-connecting us with those who have gone on.

Encouragement

In the dark with tears streaming down our faces, we stare at the screen with the huge words "THE END" frozen forever. The movie was not over. It was just beginning. The plot had not even developed. The story can't end. The relationships are left hanging in midair.

Coming to accept our own humanity and mortality in light of our loved one's death inflicts terrible pain on this grief journey. The past is gone. The present may be unbearable for you. What about the future? Can you envision being brought back together with your loved one? Is that too much to hope for?

Moving Forward

1. Reflect on your loss in light of the promise of eternal life.

2. How has the hope of heaven been helpful to you in your time of sorrow? Or has it?

3. Read and reflect on Psalm 25.

Prayer

God, forgive us for failing to do all we could to show our love for you by loving one another. Bring peace to us through your loving presence and through understanding friends. By your grace give us hope of a reunion with the ones we have lost. Amen.

54 Did God Call?

Samuel was lying down in the temple of the LORD, where the ark of God was. Then the LORD called, "Samuel! Samuel!" and he said, "Here I am!" and ran to Eli, and said, "Here I am, for you called me." But he said, "I did not call; lie down again." So he went and lay down. The LORD called again, "Samuel!" Samuel got up and went to Eli, and said, "Here I am, for you called me." But he said, "I did not call, my son; lie down again." Now Samuel did not yet know the LORD, and the word of the LORD had not yet been revealed to him. The LORD called Samuel again, a third time. And he got up and went to Eli, and said, "Here I am, for you called me."

Then Eli perceived that the LORD was calling the boy. Therefore Eli said to Samuel, "Go, lie down; and if he calls you, you shall say, 'Speak, LORD, for your servant is listening.'" So Samuel went and lay down in his place.

Now the LORD came and stood there, calling as before, "Samuel! Samuel!" And Samuel said, "Speak, for your servant is listening."
1 Samuel 3:3b-10

In this Bible story little Samuel was fast asleep in the temple where he grew up when the Lord called his name, "Samuel! Samuel!" Samuel thought it was Eli the priest calling, so he ran to answer. Eli told him to go back to bed, that he had not called him. After being awakened three times by the boy Samuel, Eli

271

understood it was the Lord speaking to little Samuel. Eli told Samuel the next time to let God know that he was listening. Then God called again "Samuel! Samuel!" Samuel said he was listening and God spoke to him.

"Samuel! Samuel!"

Had my son Samuel
Ever heard you
Calling his name?

He had grown up
In the church, too.

As with many preacher's kids
He felt the glares and stares
Of living in the fish bowl.
So he jumped out.

He swam in rivers and oceans
Far removed from
The living water
That flowed from the temple.

"Samuel" means "Name of God"
Did he know your name?

When you called to him,
"Samuel! Samuel!"
Was he listening?
Did he answer?
Was he confused
Thinking I was calling?

For awhile it had not
Seemed clear
To him
Who you are
Or

272

That you are.

He had gone from faith,
The faith of a child,
A little Samuel
Boy's trust,
To the atheism of
Young adulthood.

He did atheism proud
As only a preacher's
Kid could.
Debating philosophy,
Questioning the faith
Of any who thought
They had heard your voice,
Asking how and why
They knew.

Yet there seemed
To be occasional cracks
In the armor
Of this renegade rebel,
Remembered echoes
Of an earlier call.

This tough
Motorcycle rider
Crashed on a highway
Sliding hundreds of feet
Without a scratch,
Not what should
Have happened.

He admitted,
"Someone
(As if he did not
Know your name)
Was watching over me."

Someone had nailed
A cross above
The back door
Of the house he
Had managed
To purchase against
All odds.

He said to his girlfriend,
"Let's leave the cross there.
It probably had
Something to do
With me getting
This house."

Was that the house
You had reserved for him?
Were you calling to him
As he slept soundly there?

He rode his wild river
Over the falls
Off the edge of the earth
Into your world.

Call him now, Lord!
Awaken him now
In his new home!
"Samuel! Samuel!"

Always a heavy sleeper,
Announce with the heavenly
Trumpet that
By your grace
You have moved
Him back home
With You!

Like the prodigal son
In Jesus' parable
Has he heard
The voice of the Father?
"Welcome! Welcome home,
Samuel, my son!"

Did he see you
Running toward him
To embrace your
Wayward son?

What happens when we die? Jesus promised his disciples that his death meant that he was going away to prepare a place for them, and that he would return to take them with him to that place so that they would be together (John 14:1-7). When James, the first of the twelve disciples to die, was executed, did he see Jesus coming for him? Did he hear the Lord call him just before he was martyred?

Jesus told the repentant thief who was crucified with him, "Today you will be with me in paradise." When that thief died, did he see Jesus extend a welcoming hand to him as he entered heaven? Did he hear the voice of God saying, "Welcome, my son?"

Even though I have had eight years of theological training (M.Div. and Ph.D.) and have served more than 35 years in ordained ministry, I do not know what happens when we die. I know the theories and the Scripture (which lends itself to more than one interpretation). I don't know what happened when my son died.

People tried to comfort me by telling me what happened. "He has gone to be with God." I hoped they were right. I do the same with those who have experienced loss. Some more narrow in their theology questioned me, "Was he a believer? Was he saved?" In their theology they knew that if he was a believer, then he went (or will go) to heaven. If not, then hell is where he is (or will be). My son's death has forced me to admit that I do not know.

This loss has forced me to expand and deepen my own theology. In some ways it has become simpler and perhaps more profound. I believe that when we die, God calls us home, that the first thing we hear is God calling our name. The first thing we see is God's outstretched hand welcoming us with a huge smile on his face. The feeling we will have is that we are home, more than we have ever felt at home before—peace and joy beyond our imagination.

Encouragement

Great loss may shatter your theology. Some give up believing in God altogether. I can certainly understand that. I would encourage you to find your own answers as you ask ten thousand questions in working through your grief. No answer may come in the end. On the other hand, you may come back to believe even more strongly what you believed previously.

Grief is a terrible journey for the heart but also for the mind. We have to make sense of it. We have to find meaning in it. That's what we do as humans. In the struggle to comprehend the death of your loved one, you may gain glimpses of insight. You may even find some peace of mind. It may take months or years to get there. May God bring you peace.

Moving Forward

1. Write down the conclusions that others give to you about your loved one's death. Beside each interpretation of death, write your own critique, agreement, or disagreement.

2. What image comes to mind when you think of a loving God welcoming your loved one? Where would it take place? What would God actually say? Talk with a pastor or trusted friend about what you envision.

3. Read and reflect on Luke 15:11-32 (Parable of the Prodigal Son).

Prayer

Lord, in the teaching of Jesus Christ you command us to love. In his death you demonstrate your love for us. In his resurrection you give us hope that those we have loved and lost may live again. We don't understand all that it means, but we put our trust in you, that there is more to life, death, and love than we know. Amen.

55 Where Have You Gone, My Son?

*A writing of King Hezekiah of Judah, after he had been sick and had
recovered from his sickness:
I said: In the noontide of my days
I must depart;
I am consigned to the gates of Sheol
for the rest of my years.
I said, I shall not see the LORD
in the land of the living;
I shall look upon mortals no more
among the inhabitants of the world.
My dwelling is plucked up and removed from me
like a shepherd's tent;
like a weaver I have rolled up my life;
he cuts me off from the loom;
from day to night you bring me to an end;
I cry for help until morning;
like a lion he breaks all my bones;
from day to night you bring me to an end.*
Isaiah 38:9-13

Hezekiah reflected on his thoughts when it looked like he was
going to die of an illness, from which he was later healed. The
ancient Hebrews thought that at death one goes to a place called
"Sheol." Everyone went there, good and bad, king and peasant. It

was a place where you "slept with your ancestors." It was not eternal life. It was being cut off from life.

Where do we think our loved ones go when they die? Some assume there is no "going." Our bodies simply decay without any afterlife. Questions of afterlife often plague us when we lose someone we love. We want our loved one to be in heaven. We want to know. Our anguish over our loss sends our questions spiraling out of control.

Where are you?

Where have you gone?
Motorcycle and mountain,
Meeting, crashing,
Taking you,
Robbing us.
In an instant you were gone.
But where have you gone, My Son, My Son?

Your body lies ready for your girlfriend to view.
An "ID viewing" they call it.
Today at Four,
Just fifteen minutes — no more.
Tough, tough time for her
And for us.
I would not go to see you there,
Because the you I know is gone.
Where have you gone, My Son, My Son?

We are coming, though
To where you are,
Or where you were,
Coming to LA, to pick up what is left of your life
To pick up your ashes,
To pick up your clothes,
To pick up the pieces,
As if we could.
But where will you be?

Are you in heaven, that place with God?
As if there is a place for Him.
Did you have faith in Jesus Christ?
The faith you professed so long ago?
Or were there more questions than answers?

Have you joined Jesus and the thief in paradise?
Did you feed the hungry and clothe the naked?
So that would be enough for the King to welcome you,
So said Jesus.

What were you thinking when you crashed that canyon wall?
Or was there time to think at all?
Is there thought where you are?
Was Plato right? That all there is, is the idea?
Should we rejoice that your soul has been released
From the material prison that bound you?

Is this the land of shadows?
Or is that where you are now
The netherworld, Sheol of the Hebrew text,
"Sleeping" with Tina and Papa and Gigi,
With Len and Doug and more?

Are you more alive than we,
Dancing in that world of Spirits,
Long ago released into the Lord's Love?

Where have you gone, my Son, my Son?

Not here with us,
Thus the pain.
Not here with us,
Broken hearts,
Shattered dreams
Splintered lives.

Not here with us.

279

My mind was burdened by the question of my son's eternal destiny. It was natural for a pastor whose job it is to guide people to God, to get people to look beyond the material to the spiritual. His death challenged all my views, made me re-think and question everything. Eventually the hope of being with my son in eternity brought me comfort in the midst of the pain of losing him.

Encouragement

The thought of eventually joining your loved one in the afterlife may bring you comfort. I hope it does. Many do not want to think about that. All they can think about is the sense of absence, that their loved one is gone. You may have doubts about long-held beliefs. You may need to rethink your theology. You may not want to hear about "heaven" when you feel like you are going through hell. In fact, you may become angry when people talk about the one you lost being in heaven. It's your journey. You have to get through this any way you can.

Moving Forward

1. Talk to a friend about what you hope has happened to your loved one or about your frustration with people who keep talking about the afterlife.

2. Write a description of what heaven would be like if it were your ideal place.

3. Read the lyrics, sing or listen to the song "Hymn of Promise," by Natalie Sleeth.

Prayer

Lord, we believe in you. We admit we do not know what it is like to be with you in eternity. What does it mean to be in your presence without time, without space, or without matter? We pray that if there is a place with you beyond this life, that our loved one is there and that we will join you in infinity. Amen.

56 Sea of Glass

Coming from the throne are flashes of lightning, and rumblings and peals of thunder, and in front of the throne burn seven flaming torches, which are the seven spirits of God; and in front of the throne there is something like a sea of glass, like crystal.
Revelation 4:5-6a

The Revelation of John contains glimpses of his vision of what heaven is like. God's presence is represented in brilliant light and precious stones. Lighting and thunder show God's power. Flames of fire signify God's spirit.

A sea of glass lies before the throne. A sea before God's throne fascinates me partly because the Jews were not sailors. In most of the literature of Israel, the sea represents evil and chaos. In fact at the end of Revelation, John portrays the new heaven and the new earth without a sea. "Then I saw a new heaven and a new earth; for the first heaven and the first earth had passed away, and the sea was no more." (Rev. 21:1). Sailing was something my son and I enjoyed, so I am happy for the reference to the crystal sea before the throne of God.

Sailing the Crystal Sea

Does this young sailor
Whose dream was to sail

281

Around this world
Now sail the
Beauty of paradise
With you, Lord?

A sea of glass
Far beyond anything
In this creation
Light years past
Our imagination.

When I arrive,
I watch as he glides
By your holy throne
Waving to you on high.

An approving puff of wind
Fill his sails
As he speeds through
Living water.

I call from the shore
As he sails his boat
On the crystal sea,
"Samuel! Samuel!"

I smile with pride
As he skillfully
Tacks his sailboat
Toward me.

A beam reach
Brings him
Full sails, to me.
He drops canvas
As his boat glides
Softly to the dock.

I ask,

"Permission to come aboard
O captain, my son!"

He says,
"Permission granted, Dad.
That's what grace is all about."

And we laugh.

I step aboard.
We embrace
For what seems like days
Making up for years.

I become aware that
We are not alone.

Two men with beards
Like my son's
Come up from the cabin.

One carries
Fresh baked bread
The other brings a
Bottle of wine.

"Dad, let me introduce
You to Pete and John."
I stammer and stutter
"You mean . . . ?"

Pete gives me a
Big bear hug
While John slaps me
On the back
"Welcome aboard!"
They say,
"We've been expecting you."

283

"Much nicer than the Sea of Galilee,
Don't you think, Sam?"
Pete asks.

I can only nod.

"No storms here,"
Adds John,
"Always fair winds."

"Fine sailor, this son of yours,"
Pete offers,
"You taught him well."

"Thanks,"
I manage.

Samuel grins at me,
Winks and shouts,
"Hoist the main!"

I wrap the sheet
Around the winch
Crank to raise the mainsail.

The sail fills
With a following breeze as
We gently glide away
From the dock.

Pete unfurls the jib.
John cleats it off.
Samuel finesses the wheel
As the pristine water
Gurgles along the hull.

We relax in the cockpit
Eat and drink
Laughing together

Friends
Sailing the crystal sea.

When I think about heaven in light of my son's death, I cry. Sometimes I am afraid we will not see each other again. Other times I am more hopeful that we will be reunited. Joy and sorrow mix with my tears as I imagine what it will be like to be together with him in the presence of our loving God. Many emotions collide as I think about God, my son, and eternity.

Encouragement

What will heaven be like? In the Book of Revelation we have a poetic and apocalyptic vision, which is not to be taken literally of course. I like what one of my parishioners said about Revelation. He said, "I don't understand Revelation when I read it, but it makes me feel good." I assured him that he had probably understood it better than he realized.

The message of the Revelation is that God wins in the end. It's a book about the vision of God's victory and victory for the people of God. God overcomes death and sin. Evil and cruelty will come to an end. Oppression and injustice will no longer be part of our experience. Neither will death. In light of your loss, I hope you can come to a vision of eternal peace for those you have lost and for yourself.

Moving Forward

1. Talk with a friend or family member about what you hope heaven would be for your loved one.

2. List the five things your loved one would want to do in heaven. What would you enjoy doing with him or her?

3. Read and reflect on Revelation 21:1-4.

Prayer

God of eternity, we long to be with the ones we have lost. We ask that you would give us faith to believe in your grace for them and for us. Help us see beyond this world into the glory of your eternal presence. When our vision is blurred because tears fill our eyes and our hearts, wipe away our tears as we trust in you. Amen.

GRATITUDE & HOPE

57 A Broken but Grateful Heart

Give thanks in all circumstances; for this is the will of God in Christ Jesus for you.
1 Thessalonians 5:18

I do not interpret this verse to mean that everything that happens to us is exactly what our Lord Jesus would desire for us, what God would will for us. That would mean that God inflicts terrible pain on some people for no apparent reason. Rather the will of God is that we are always grateful. It is certainly not easy to be grateful when we are grieving. The two previous verses also give what might appear like unreasonable commands: "Rejoice always, pray without ceasing." (1 Thess. 5:16-17). Yet I have found that in giving thanks healing begins.

I have prayed at funerals for decades, "Lord, may gratitude for the gift you gave us in _____ (deceased's name) help heal our hearts and minds." I have been convinced that gratitude is central to handling grief—for other people. Being grateful is a key in the healing process. What about for me?

Be Grateful!

When my heart

286

Is shattered,
All I can think about
Is my loss.

My son is gone.
I will never
Get him back.
The longing and
Heartache are
Unbearable.

Then the Pastor's voice
Inside me says,
"Be grateful."

"Grateful?" I shout back.
"Grateful that my son is gone?"

Then whispered softly
By the battalions of vacant hearts,
Of broken men who had longed
For sons,
"Grateful that you had a son."

"What you lost we never had.
What you gained,
Even if only for a while,
We would have treasured.
Be grateful!"

From lonely souls
Of angry men
Gone now from sight
I hear a rusty rebuke.

"You have your daughter.
You have your wife.
You have your God.
You had your son.

Be grateful!
We had none."

From thousands,
Ten thousands of
Those who fought
In fatal wars
Who knew the love
Of ma and pa.

But never knew the
Joy of a loving wife
Who never held her
In their arms,
Who never knew the thrill
Of holding their tiny newborn
Daughter or son.

Their voices mingle
In mild rebuke,
"Be grateful!"

Frustrated couples
Whose love is no less
Profound though no
Child is born to testify
Join the chorus,

"We who live in a barren land
Mourn your loss of an orchard.
Not just the tree, but the fruit
Which may have come from his life."

In our desert
We know not the loss
But the absence.
So we console and encourage
"Be grateful!"

Then from the throne
High above
I hear a sad and solemn voice,
"I lost my Son, too.
Be grateful!"

I do not expect people at a funeral to be overwhelmed with gratitude for the beloved whom God brought into their lives, who is now gone. My goal in that prayer of gratitude is to plant a seed in their hearts and minds that will grow into gratefulness. In South Florida the vast majority of bulletins or programs have the title "A Celebration of the Life of _____," instead of, "In Memory of _____." That's what most families want nowadays. Some of my clergy friends say it's not right. To focus on celebrating a person's life does not acknowledge the loss and depth of grief. I personally think it's a good thing if a family wants to celebrate their loved one's life in the funeral or memorial service. It moves in the direction of being grateful.

We did the same for our son's service bulletin. At my son's service I was not feeling gratitude but shock, anger, and sadness. After months of grieving, gratitude is growing in my heart. When I give thanks to God for my son, I am acknowledging his presence in my life for 32 years as a blessing from God. Instead of focusing on my loss, I am grateful for what I gained in having had a son, for the privilege of being his father. At times sadness still overwhelms me. Yet there are moments now when I can celebrate my son's life in a prayer of gratitude to God. Such gratitude helps heal my broken heart.

Encouragement

I encourage you to be grateful for the one you have loved and lost. In grief we focus on our loss. That is natural and normal—especially in the early days, weeks and months. Sow a little gratitude in the plowed soil of your broken heart. Gratefulness will grow to give you strength to go on.

Moving Forward

1. Write a list of the things you are grateful for about the one you lost. Keep the list and add to it as you remember things you are thankful for.

2. Read and reflect Psalm 100.

Prayer

Lord, we are grateful that you gave us our loved one, whom we had the privilege of knowing and loving. Though we wish with every fiber of our being that our beloved would not have died, we are still grateful. We pray that all we do today will show our gratitude to you and honor the memory of the one we miss so much. For those of us in the throes of grief, help gratitude to creep into our hearts and minds to begin to heal us. Amen.

58 Better to Have Loved and Lost?

Cursed be the day
on which I was born!
The day when my mother bore me,
let it not be blessed!
Cursed be the man
who brought the news to my father, saying,
"A child is born to you, a son,"
making him very glad.
Let that man be like the cities
that the LORD overthrew without pity;
let him hear a cry in the morning
and an alarm at noon,
because he did not kill me in the womb;
so my mother would have been my grave,
and her womb forever great.
Why did I come forth from the womb
to see toil and sorrow,
and spend my days in shame?
Jeremiah 20:14-18

God told Jeremiah not to marry so that he would not have a child. "The word of the LORD came to me: You shall not take a wife, nor shall you have sons or daughters in this place." (Jeremiah 16:1-2)

Why was he given this command? Because judgment was to come on Israel according to the word of the Lord given to Jeremiah. All children born then were going to die of starvation in the siege against Jerusalem or be slaughtered by Babylonian soldiers. In that context, would it be better to have brought a child into the world, to have loved and lost? Is God's advice to Jeremiah the wisest?

I've heard couples, who have chosen to be childless, say that they did not want to bring a child into such a violent world as ours. That has always seemed to me to be such a negative view of the world. Yet people's experience of life may justify not having children because of what they have had to suffer and their desire to prevent children from that pain. Jeremiah's insight into the immediate future of his city would seem to bolster the wisdom of remaining childless.

Friends of mine had been trying to have a child for many years. After several failed attempts with the latest scientific methods, their only option was to adopt a child. They were very disappointed but knew that there are children who need good adoptive parents.

Is the choice to bear or raise children a selfish choice? Are the maternal and paternal instincts part of our DNA? It is true that the only one of God's commandments we have kept is, "...Be fruitful and multiply, and fill the earth..."(Genesis 1:28) On the whole we have done that well, but not everyone gets that opportunity or wants it.

When you lose a child, would it have been better not to have brought him into the world for his sake? If she suffered greatly, was our choice to have her a wrong one? These questions have no answers, like so many questions when parents lose a son or daughter.

These questions tend to produce guilt in us as parents that we could not protect the ones we loved so much from suffering. When it comes to those of us who are left behind, whose hearts are broken, do we agree with Tennyson that it is better to have loved and lost than never to have loved at all? A spouse, a lover, a sister, a brother, a friend, all of us who have experienced loss, may come to that question as well. Each of us who has experienced grief, wrestles with that question.

Better to Have Loved

Better to have loved and lost
Than never to have loved at all!
The poet's conclusion
At the loss of a friend.

How can I judge the value
Of my broken heart?
The greater the love
The greater the grief?
Would it not be better
To love less?
To hurt less?

Would not the prophylaxis
Of a distant heart
Have prevented this brokenness?
Is there no anesthesia against
The pain of love?
Is it better to have lived and
Died than never to have lived?

The prophet laments
His mother's womb
Had not been his grave.
The stillborn has the advantage
Over those of us who survive
For heartache, suffering, and death.

But what do the prophet and poet know?
Jesus said, "Love one another."
But if we do, we will be broken
Again
And again
And again.

The one we cradled

293

Crushed.
The one we held so tightly
Snatched away.

In the end I side
With Tennyson
Better broken by love
Than to remain whole
Without it.

Human wholeness can only come
After being shattered
By a grief born out of love.

And love?
Our only reason
For being.

For me, I am grateful to have loved my son and been loved by him. I wish away his death every day, wishing it had never happened, wishing that his life had not ended. But I cannot wish away the life he had. Even in all my pain and all the things my son suffered, I cannot agree with the prophet Jeremiah. Neither my son nor I would have been better if he'd never been born.

Encouragement

You may hurt so much that you wish you had never been born, like the prophet Jeremiah. If you endured the suffering of a loved one, you may have wished they had never been born. Negative thoughts pounce on us day after day in our grief. Depression is a normal reaction to loss. You may need help in getting through this time. Be open to the possibility of talking to someone about your loss and your negative thoughts. I met with a counselor for several months to help me.

Moving Forward

1. If your deep sadness is interfering with your ability to function normally, see a psychologist, psychiatrist, mental health counselor

or pastoral counselor to help you through depression that comes with grief.

2. If you have thoughts of suicide, that is normal. If you think of ways you might end your life, please get help before you act on those thoughts.

3. Sing, read the lyrics aloud or play the hymn "Abide with Me," by Henry Francis Lyte.

4. Read and reflect on Psalm 16.

Prayer
Thank you, Lord, for the one we loved and lost. We are grateful for the love we had for them and their love for us, even though that makes our pain greater. Thank you for loving us through the pain. We love you, Lord. Amen.

59 They Are No More

Thus says the LORD:
A voice is heard in Ramah,
lamentation and bitter weeping.
Rachel is weeping for her children;
she refuses to be comforted for her children,
because they are no more.
Thus says the LORD:
Keep your voice from weeping,
and your eyes from tears;
for there is a reward for your work, says the LORD:
they shall come back from the land of the enemy;
there is hope for your future, says the LORD:
your children shall come back to their own country.
Jeremiah 31:15-17

The prophet Jeremiah describes "Rachel" weeping for her children who are "no more." The poet portrays Israel as a mother who mourns her children being killed or taken captive. The historical context is the defeat of Israel at the hands of Babylon. The Babylonians took most of the survivors to Babylon as slaves. Through the voice of God, the prophet encourages mother "Rachel" not to mourn because they will return.

When a parent leaves a young child, the child often cries. It's called separation anxiety. When we were in missionary training, getting ready to separate our children from their grandparents (the real unpardonable sin), we were taught that separation for the child is like death. The child has no grasp on the abstract future and so to be separated is to be no more in the child's view. It is an emotional loss, which we adults see as temporary, but the child does not understand they are not gone forever. Is it the same with us when someone dies?

When their heart stops beating, when there are no brain waves, it is so difficult to accept that the end has come. Perhaps nothing is harder in life than to come to terms with the loss of someone we love. Grief is the horrible process of learning to live with the loss. We want to hang on to hope, which seems impossible when "they are no more."

Terminal, Terminus

It seems stupid
To everyone else
To have
Hope
When this battle
Has dragged on
So long.

But she will
Get better.
I know she will.

She will
Pull through.
The doctors
Don't know.

Only God knows.
Everybody's praying.
God will heal.
He has to.

They say

297

I need to accept the end.
I need to let go,
To resign myself.

I refuse.

As long as her heart
Is beating
My hope
Throbs.

As long as her
Lungs keep filling
I will not
Exhale this
Longing for life.

With every rise of
Her chest
My confidence
Lifts on the
Wave of tomorrow.

They say only
Days, hours maybe
For death to come.

"Terminal" is such
An ugly word
To describe
Someone I love.

Who made them
Judge and jury?
Lords of
The universe?

They do not
Give life.

How can they know
When the Giver will
Take it?

There has to be
More.
This cannot be
The end.

Oh no!
The line is flat.
The alarm on the
Machine blares.

She is gone.

The nurse confirms.
"Write it down,"
She says to the other.
Looking at the clock
Then her watch
"8:27."

This cannot be the end.
Her love cannot stop
It cannot end.
The power of her love for us
And our love for her
Cannot stop on a dime.
It must go on.

Terminal
Has to mean
That she has
Caught another flight
That she was lifted
From the tarmac of earth
To the altitude of another realm.

Give me hope that this is
Not all there is.
She cannot end.
There was nothing
Terminal about her.

Her topsail has disappeared
From my horizon.
Give me faith
To believe
Others are getting
Excited as they see her
Flag flying
Above the waves.

I drift toward them
In her wake
Wishing a great
Wind would push me
Up alongside her
So I could attach
My barnacled self
To her hull.

A shift of wind
Would carry us
To another adventure
Another port.

Her chest lies still.
Her skin grows cool.
Her eyes do not flutter
Behind the veils of skin.

The Spirit has carried
Her to distant shores
Where they speak
A language of love
Beyond my comprehension

A language she had already mastered.

Love has no terminus.
Love has no end.

Shock and denial are said to be the first aspects of our experience in grief. So I learned in psychology classes. They are called psychological defenses, ways our minds protect us as we recoil from the reality before us. Initially we cannot believe that death has come, that "they are no more." It seems to be a lie our brains just cannot accept.

So we deny that it is real, which can make you feel crazy. Part of you knows it is true. But emotionally it is beyond comprehension. Being in shock and denying reality are normal, even though it seems crazy—to ourselves and especially to those who have not gone through the nightmare of loss.

Encouragement
There is hope for the future. You will get through this. You do not want to accept the harsh reality of what has happened. You may find ways to deny that it has happened, but the reality of death will keep slapping you in the face until you move into full-blown mourning. Grief tortures us into submitting to the reality, which has conquered our spirits. Yet there is hope beyond death.

Moving Forward
1. If you have a bulletin or program from a funeral or memorial service, read over every detail, date of birth, date of death, and so on, asking for God's help as you read.

2. When you are able, hold the container of ashes in your hands or visit the grave, praying for God to help you accept the reality of what has happened, even though that is the last thing you want to do.

3. Read and reflect on Psalm 39.

Prayer
God of grace and mercy, help us to accept the harsh reality of our loss. As we grieve, aid us in acknowledging what our hearts and minds do not

want to admit, that death has come. Hold us close as we come to grips with our loss. Do not let us drown in this sea of emotions. Amen.

60 Happy New Year?

Like vinegar on a wound
is one who sings songs to a heavy heart.
Like a moth in clothing or a worm in wood,
sorrow gnaws at the human heart.
Proverbs 25:20

Happy New Year! I certainly hope it is happier than last year—not that there were not happy times. But the losses so overwhelm the memory of the happiness. The first New Year after the loss of someone you love deeply brings a mixture of feelings. I am happy to let go of last year hoping we will not have to deal with any more losses. "Good riddance!" to the pain of that year.

Yet I also feel a longing to hang on to last year. If I let go, won't I lose something of my son? As the memories of his death become more distant, won't part of what he meant to me disappear? As my suffering becomes more bearable, is the loss less real? Am I somehow being less a father to him, less loyal to him, because I have now moved on to a New Year? He is now even further away from me. As time marches forward and never looks back, I hear the echo of Jesus' harsh words, "Let the dead bury their dead!" (Matthew 8:28)

Happy New Year?

His bloody sword raised in the air
Death marches forward
Never looking back at the devastation
Of the fields of bodies
Once alive

No stopping to honor dead
Or moments of silence out of respect
For the remaining
Only reaping
And weeping
From behind

Right and left
They fall
Hunger, Cancer
Heart attack, Suicide
Bombs, Tsunamis
Earthquakes, Gang rape
Pneumonia, Stroke
Cars, motorcycles crashing
Drones, missiles attacking
Murders, AIDS
Hurricanes, Tornadoes

Never winded
He does not pause
A vast arsenal
Blood clot
Massive explosion
Arctic cold
Extreme heat
Burned out battlefields

He wields his weapons
Through crowded humanity
Unaffected by

Wails in his wake
Unslowed by human longing
To hang on to last year
For one more day,
Even one more hour,
One more conversation,
A chance to say
What could have been said
Should have been
Would have
Had we known
Death would come?

Weapon of choice?
Coroner must decide
Cause of death,
When life ended.

Dragged into this New Year
Longing for the loved ones we have lost
Whose lives were left behind
In last year
Forever so labeled
In obituaries
Mortuaries
Cemeteries
While we
Unwillingly
Move on

Shackled to the Conqueror
Who bulldozes
Through the living
Filling mass graves

But eventually
Cuts our chains
Leaving us
Forever to remain

In last year.

The New Year brings mixed emotions—grief and hope. Each passing milestone, such as the anniversary of his death or a birthday, takes me further away from the last time I talked with him. Time distances me from him even more, compounding the loss.

I remember when I taught him to sail a dingy. As he caught the wind and glided away from me, he moved farther and farther away. I was worried that he might not maneuver the tack and gibe to bring him back to me. He managed just fine. But now he is gone. Time blows all the events of his life further and further away. Yet I feel hopeful with a new year that perhaps the pain will diminish, that no more deaths will come on us. I am learning to live with the loss and the movement of time. Even against my will I am beginning to accept it.

Encouragement

I do not believe that time heals all wounds. But with time, healing will take place in your life. Your loss will get easier to live with. Grief never completely goes away. But its presence becomes less overwhelming, less oppressive with time. Yes, it seems to take forever for that to happen. You may not believe it now, but it will get better. The pain of your loss will become less acute. You can learn to live with what has happened. Life can go on.

Moving Forward

1. Read and reflect on Ecclesiastes 3:1-8.

2. Holidays are difficult when dealing with loss. Anticipate how hard it may be and plan to do what will be most helpful for you. Plan to spend time with family or friends, or to be alone, whichever helps. Recognize that you may be especially sad during times when others are rejoicing.

3. Do something on a holiday to remember your loved one in a way that is meaningful. Start a new tradition or preserve an old one.

Prayer

O God, with you there is no time, or there is all time. What do we, who are bound by the ticking clock, know? All we know is now. We pray that whatever has been and whatever will be is with you, and that you are with us, now for all time. Amen.

61 Those Who Have No Hope

But we do not want you to be uninformed, brothers and sisters, about those who have died, so that you may not grieve as others do who have no hope. For since we believe that Jesus died and rose again, even so, through Jesus, God will bring with him those who have died.
1 Thessalonians 4:13-14

St. Paul wrote these words to early Christians who had thought that the return of Christ was imminent. They had a crisis of faith because Jesus Christ had not appeared and some of their Christian family and friends had died. That is not what was supposed to happen. So Paul explained that, as Christians, our hope is that our loved ones will live again. Our grief is not the same as someone who has no hope of ever reuniting with their lost loved ones. Christian hope is important as we mourn.

Ring of Hope

I can't make out
The writing
On this piece of
Styrofoam
We cling to,
Our rescue
From drowning

308

Too tired to swim
Another stroke

Don't know
The direction
Anyway

The ship is gone
And most on board
Though we cannot
Be sure in the dark.

The weeping waves
Break over us
But we clamp our
Lives on this bit
Of polystyrene
To survive.

Another comes
Crashing over us
Slapping me with
A mouthful of salty brine.

I panic.
Is she gone?
Has she been knocked
Off the life ring?

The wave washes
Away.
She is still there
Clinging with me
To this ring of hope.

All else is lost
Except this circle
Of hope.

We barely make out
The heads of others
Bobbing in this
Mourning sea.

Some disappear
Beneath the surface
And do not come back
Up for air, for life.

We hear muffled
Calls for help,
Wails
When a child
Slips the grasp
Of mom or dad.

I wish we could get this
Life ring
To them.
We could all
Hold on
Together.

My wife and I
Lock arms
On this tiny
Raft of faith.

As the black
Gives way to gray
We are alone.

Only this bit of belief
Has kept us together
Kept us alive
Keeps us now.

My heart and mind keep coming back to the bedrock of our faith—because of Jesus Christ there is hope of life beyond the grave. Because of the life, death, and resurrection of Christ Jesus, death is not the end, but the beginning of a new adventure with God. I keep returning to this truth in the dark times of my grief.

I try to imagine what my son might be doing in heaven. I picture him with those friends and family we have lost before and since his death. Is he rocking our friends' babies who died? Is he listening to music with our friends' son? Is he fishing with his cousin who died a year after he did? Is he listening to stories with his aunt Tina or his Uncle Len? Sometimes I think this helps. Other times it seems to make me sadder. But in the end this hope in Christ is what I cling to.

Encouragement

Many of us have different ideas about life and death. The Christian promise of life after death may provide you some comfort. It's not what you want. You want your loved one back with you now. In our anger or sadness, we don't want to hear about the afterlife. Our grief is in this life. Yet the hope of being with your loved one again may be a life ring as you struggle to stay afloat in your sea of grief.

Moving Forward

1. Make a list of all those you hope your loved one will be with in heaven.

2. Reflect on what your loved one might be doing in the afterlife. What would she or he want to do?

3. Read and reflect on Romans 8:18-25 and what it means to be "saved by hope."

Prayer

God of hope, fill us with the expectancy that this is not all there is to life. In our loss, help us to see beyond the horizon of this temporal bubble to eternity. Grant us the peace of knowing that our loved one is in your loving arms. Amen.

62 Looking Forward to Easter

Now if Christ is proclaimed as raised from the dead, how can some of you say there is no resurrection of the dead? If there is no resurrection of the dead, then Christ has not been raised; and if Christ has not been raised, then our proclamation has been in vain and your faith has been in vain. We are even found to be misrepresenting God, because we testified of God that he raised Christ – whom he did not raise if it is true that the dead are not raised. For if the dead are not raised, then Christ has not been raised. If Christ has not been raised, your faith is futile and you are still in your sins. Then those also who have died in Christ have perished. If for this life only we have hoped in Christ, we are of all people most to be pitied.
1 Corinthians 15:12-19

St. Paul is correct. The Christian faith hinges on the resurrection of Jesus Christ. If Jesus was not raised from the dead, then the hope of Easter is a sham. Christians would be guilty of misrepresenting God, as Paul argues, if God did not raise Jesus from the dead. The resurrection is the basis for the early church believing that Jesus was the Son of God, and that his death atoned for our sins. Without Easter there is no hope for eternal life. We Christians believe that Jesus was raised from death and have hope that we will be raised to eternal life with Christ.

I'm looking forward to Easter this year in a way that I have not previously. Our son's death last May has shaken me to the core. I look forward to the healing that Easter brings, the hope of life beyond, the triumph of life over death—God's putting a comma, where death had placed a period. I want to hang on to that promise of life beyond death.

"Wait! There's more!"

I abandon my bed and
Drag my carcass
To the easy chair.
At least something
Should be easy.

Grief has robbed
Me of sleep again.
I turn on the mindless
Chatter of late night
Infomercials.

The hawker breaks into
My fog for an instant.
"Wait! There's more!"
Irritating sales ploy
To get me to buy
Something to clutter my
Garage.

They always
Promise more
But deliver less
Of anything important.

I want more
I want my son back.

Is the church
Like the late
Night huckster
Offering Easter hope

313

Every Sunday?

"Wait! Don't despair!
There's more!

Then on Easter
The pastor preaches the
Empty tomb.
Easter Lilies
Envelope the
Brass quartet.
Organ music fills the
Packed sanctuary.

All anxious to hear
"Wait! There's more!"
Eager to believe
Easter hope.

Without it
The screen goes
Blank.

Without it
Death
Reigns forever.

Without it
The darkness
Wins.

Without it
Why go on?

The celebration of Easter has new meaning for me since my son's death. More than any other loved one's death, I have longed for this hope of life with him again. The resurrection of Jesus gives me that hope. Not only that I will be able to be with my son, but also my sister, my grandparents, my brothers-in-law, my wife's parents, and friends who have died throughout the years. I will meet my grandfather, who died when my father was only 11 years old.

Every year my list gets longer of people I've lost. For me, death would eventually rob this life of all meaning. Without this hope of eternal life what is the point? Indeed, I've known people who have lost hope and taken their lives because of deep grief. How tragic! That is why the good news of Jesus Christ speaks to me. God's promise of eternal life brings me hope in the valley of my despair. Easter rolls the stone away from the tomb of my depression. Easter shines into the darkness of my doubt.

Encouragement

You have lost someone you love, which is the most painful experience we have as humans. When someone says, "Don't worry, you will see them again," your reaction may run the gamut from anger to disbelief. Anger fills you because you want the person back with you now. Doubt assails you because it sounds too good to be true, like "pie in the sky by and by." Whether it's the pastor at the funeral or a well-meaning friend, they often come across as the huckster on TV who shouts, "Wait! There's more!" You want there to be more, more shared laughter, more long conversations, more touches, more hugs, more.

It's hard to accept something we cannot see. I encourage you to consider the possibility that there is eternal life for you and for your loved one. If you doubt, be honest with your doubt and patient with yourself in this journey. It may not ease your immediate pain, yet the hope of Easter can begin to grow from a tiny seed to a tree of confidence over time. The cool shade of that resurrection tree can provide a great deal of comfort to your burned out soul.

Moving Forward

1. Read and reflect on the earliest Gospel story of the resurrection of Jesus (Mark 16:1-7).

2. Write a list of the names of those whom you have lost. Beside each name write a sentence or two of what you will say to them when you see them in the next life.

315

3. Converse with those who knew your loved one about what he or she might be doing in an ideal setting as we imagine heaven to be. (Such as fishing, painting, writing, playing tennis, drawing, cooking, golfing, singing, or dancing)

Prayer
Lord of eternity, because we believe in you, we have hope for a life beyond this life. Because you raised Jesus from the dead and promised to raise us as well, we have hope of seeing again those whom we have lost. We are grateful for this hope. May it continue to grow in our hearts and minds. Amen.

63 Blessed Be My Rock

The LORD is my rock, my fortress, and my deliverer,
my God, my rock in whom I take refuge,
my shield, and the horn of my salvation, my stronghold.
Psalm 18:2

The LORD lives! Blessed be my rock,
and exalted be the God of my salvation.
Psalm 18:46

David praised God, who had delivered him from King Saul and other enemies. He testified that in the midst of all his battles and in the face of death, God had been his rock, his stronghold and his refuge.

Although this assurance is comforting, it is often only in hindsight that we realize God has been there for us. In the midst of suffering, it is hard to sense God's presence or even to believe in God. A rabbi friend told me years after he lost his daughter, "The hardest thing is keeping one's faith."

My Rock

Death roars
Like a category five tornado
Blasting away

All man-made façades
Flattening homes in its path,
Yet you are
My Rock
My life is hidden in you.

The seas are raging
Tossing me back and forth
Tormented in a swirling sea
Of emotions,
Yet you bring me calm.

Like a car being crushed
Into a cube of metal
Grief is crushing,
Bearing in on me
From all sides,
But you make a space
For me in the palm
Of your hand.

Like a giant python
Sadness is constricting,
Squeezing the breath out of me,
Yet you breathe life
Back into me.

I wilt like
A flower in the
Desert sun,
But you are the rain
That revives my soul.

Grateful to you
I am and always
Will be.

Blessed be my Rock!

How do I know God is with me? I am surviving this grief. I have not given in to the self-destructive thoughts. I have not walked away from faith and family. Many times God has seemed light years away, even non-existent. Yet God has not absent from me, though that is what I felt. Looking back, I can see how God has been carrying me through these dark and difficult times.

Encouragement
God is there for you. Do you believe that? Do you even want to think that? You may be devastated that God did not spare your loved one. You may be angry with God. All those thoughts and feelings are normal in the midst of our grieving even for persons of faith. God does not hold our doubt and pain against us. Instead, God surrounds us like the air we breathe and supports us like the ground we walk on. God protects us, embraces us and sustains us. Though we may not want to accept his love and care in the midst of heartache, God is there for us. God is our refuge. God's unseen presence always works to bring healing to our brokenness.

Moving Forward
1. Read and reflect on Psalm 18. Write the words "Rock, Fortress, Deliverer, Refuge, Shield, Salvation, and Stronghold (18:2)." Circle the ones that you can relate to God on your journey through grief.

2. Take time to ponder the glory of God in creation by contemplating mountains, oceans, beaches, forests or even a flower. Consider how God has created and sustained creation and how God has been sustaining you even in the midst of your anguish.

Prayer
God of grace and glory, help us to believe in your love and care, even in the midst of our pain. Bring healing to us as we mourn those we have lost. Reveal yourself to us as our Rock, our Fortress, our Stronghold, our Deliverer, our Refuge, our Shield, and our Salvation. May we rise from the ashes of our grief to praise you again. Amen.

64 Door of Hope

Therefore, I will now allure her,
and bring her into the wilderness,
and speak tenderly to her.
From there I will give her her vineyards,
and make the Valley of Achor (Trouble) a door of hope.
There she shall respond as in the days of her youth,
as at the time when she came out of the land of Egypt.
On that day, says the LORD, you will call me, "My husband," and no
longer will you call me, "My Baal."
Hosea 2:14-16

The prophet Hosea is talking about God wooing Israel back from apostasy, as a husband might try to win back his estranged wife. God will transform the Valley of Trouble (Achor) into a door of hope. The Valley of Trouble (Achor) near Jericho was named as a memorial to death and defeat—the death of those who died trying to conquer the city of Ai, and the execution of those who caused the defeat. (For more on the bizarre story read Joshua 7).

Does God do that? Does God transform valleys of death and defeat into pathways to hope? If so what does it have to do with my loss? I do not want to think that good can come out of my loss. In some ways that seems disloyal to my son. It seems to justify what cannot be justified. Such rationalization offends my deep emotional pain.

Unwelcome Hope

A tiny green sprout
Springs up from
The black heart of the
Decaying stump.

The tiny stick trunk
Pushes past the
Darkened walls
Of the giant oak
Killed by a
Lightning strike.

Proud,
Claiming the crater
Of greatness remembered.
Pretentious,
Promising shade for the house
Where he had lived.

The vine of hope grows slowly
Inching its way up from
The basement of my soul
Through the open cellar door
Toward the sunlight
Across wounded fields
Creeping over broken gravestones
Shards of dreams long forgotten.

It embraces the stump,
Celebrates the seedling
Growing in the heart
Of pain and loss.

I want to
Take a machete
To this unwelcome
Growth inside me.

Kill off the good that
Would displace
My loss,
Disturb my sadness
Assuage my pain!

A ray of sunlight
Breaks through the
Leafy canopy of my
Brokenness,
Shining on
The tendrils of hope.

Hope brings no disrespect
Intends no dishonor.
When I am ready,
Hope will invite her friends
Peace and Joy to join us
As they sit with me
In silence
In the ashes of my grief.

Eventually
Hope whispers,
"It's going to be okay.
You will get through this,"
To unwilling ears.

My journey from heartbreak to hope has been rocky. At times I've wanted to give up, to resist the hope growing within me. Yet this hope is the grace of God at work restoring my soul. In the face of death, only the presence of God can bring hope to us. Only God can take us beyond heartache in this life, filling us with hope to go on now, and hope of life eternal.

Encouragement

God's grace surrounds us, works in us, and brings healing to us even when we are unaware of it. It's a gentle process in which

322

God's love mends our broken hearts. Only God can take that which is the worst in life—death—and bring hope. Hope, like a seedling, takes root in the midst of death and decay.

This kind of hope only grows in gardens of despair. It is God's gift to those of us who grieve deeply. Hope saves us from the depths of loss, enabling us eventually to stand. My prayer is that this hope finds you and that you can embrace it and be empowered by it to go on.

Moving Forward

1. Plant a tree in memory of your loved one.

2. Make a contribution to a charity in the name of your loved one.

3. Memorialize your loved one through art: write a poem, compose a song, paint a painting, or make a sculpture.

4. Buy a memorial plaque or brick with the name of your loved one in a church or charitable organization.

5. 1 Timothy 1:1 begins, "Paul, an apostle of Christ Jesus by the command of God our Savior and of Christ Jesus our hope." What does it mean to you that Jesus Christ is our hope?

Prayer

God of grace, grant us hope for today and for tomorrow. When we are overwhelmed with grief, allow the seed of hope to grow in us so that we can go on. When everything inside us is limp with fatigue, strengthen us so we will have the energy and the will to continue this difficult journey. Amen.

323

65 Blessed Are Those who Mourn

"Blessed are those who mourn, for they will be comforted."
Matthew 5:4

Then I saw a new heaven and a new earth; for the first heaven and the first earth had passed away, and the sea was no more. And I saw the holy city, the new Jerusalem, coming down out of heaven from God, prepared as a bride adorned for her husband. And I heard a loud voice from the throne saying,
"See, the home of God is among mortals.
He will dwell with them as their God;
they will be his peoples,
and God himself will be with them;
he will wipe every tear from their eyes.
Death will be no more;
mourning and crying and pain will be no more,
for the first things have passed away."
Revelation 21:1-4

Coffer of Grace

The day he died
The steel box
Glowing red with heat
Crashed into my chest.

324

I caught it
With my hands.
Part instinct
Part self-defense.

The force of the
Basketball-sized box
Knocked me off my feet
Flat on my back and
Welded
The open container
To my chest.

The skin of my hands
Melted onto the metal,
My heart seared by the steel,
My insides boiled.

Eventually I manage to stand.
In agony
I scream for God
To take away this pain
From the core of my being.

My tears stream into
The hole in the
In the center of the
Concave top
Turning the heated metal cold.

I thrash and twist
Trying to free myself.
Bucked like the rider on
An angry bull
The steel chest
Sloshes my tears
Left and right
Round and round.

Is that why it's affixed to me?
To catch my tears?

I survive.
I feel like a freak
Hands fixed to the
Sides of this burnt box.
No one
Notices.

My skin has grown around it.
It has become part of me.

I cannot throw it off
Pull it way
Part with it.

I pray constantly for God to
Perform surgery,
To remove
This metal coffin,
Constant reminder
Of my loss.

Why should I be burdened
For the rest of my life?
Why should this gray receptacle
Come between us?
What possible purpose
Could this container serve?

I resign myself
To carry this
Casket of grief,
A pallbearer for
My own sadness.
The chest moves
Up and down
With each sigh.

326

Finally after
Many months
The box is filled to the brim
With tears.

It begins to sink
Into my chest.
My fingers are set free
One by one
As the salty crate
Disappears within me.

What is happening?
Won't this kill me?

Then God speaks,
"This is a coffer of grace.
These are not only your tears,
But also mine.

The box could only
Become part of you
When it was filled with tears
We have cried together
As I have held you.

Now that
Our tears have
Blended together,
This coffer of grace
Envelopes your heart.

Put your burned hand
Into my scarred hand
As we fill the
Coffers of others with
Grace
Compassion

327

Love,
With our Tears."

"Blessed are those who mourn, for they will be comforted." (Matthew 5:4) It's one of the strangest statements Jesus ever made. Happy are those who mourn? What kind of blessing do these tears bring? "…For they will be comforted." Really? Would it not be better to have not lost the one we loved? Far better, far more blessed!

Jesus' words baffle our logical minds. How are the desolate happy? How are those struggling with deep sadness blessed? Would it not be better to avoid this pain in the first place? Isn't that what it means to be blessed — not to suffer?

Grief pounces on us and we have no escape. Our only hope when tragedy strikes is to get through it, to survive. God wants much more for us than that. With God there is more.

That is what this book has been about. It is about confronting the pain, admitting the heartache, living through the suffering, acknowledging that through it all, the Lord walks with us, even if we do not believe in God, even if we do not sense God's presence.

Jesus said that those of us who mourn will be comforted. The verb "comfort" in Greek is parakaleo, which means at its root "to call alongside." When we mourn, we need someone to come alongside us. God promises to comfort us by walking hand in hand with us.

My purpose in sharing my struggles in this book has been first to give you permission to grieve. It's okay to cry, to weep, to be sad, for as long as it takes. In fact, grieving a devastating loss will never end, but will become more tolerable.

Second, by sharing bits of my journey, I want to give you hope, not only the hope of eternal life, which may seem distant and irrelevant to you now, but the hope that you can and will get through this. What you are experiencing may be the worst pain you have ever felt. I will not lie to you. It never goes away completely. Yet you will learn to live with it. In spite of your heartache, you will come to know joy and peace again.

Third, I write as a witness to the grace of God. It has taken me a long time to be able to be a witness for God's grace in grief. God has been with me every step of the way, but when I was going through denial, anger, and deep sadness, it was hard to be aware of God's presence, difficult to even believe in a God who cared. After more than two years, I am beginning to see this journey as a gift, one I would never ask for, an unwanted and unwelcomed gift.

Could this "dark night of the soul," as St. John of the Cross called it, be a path to something positive? No, I am not saying that God caused your loss or mine. I would not blame God for all the tragedies that happen to people. That would make God into a horrible beast. Nor am I suggesting that your loss or mine broke us so that in the end we would be better people. There is no "silver lining" to loss. Rather, because of who God is, loving and compassionate, we who grieve get special attention. God walks with us because we desperately need God.

The God we see in Jesus is always compassionate, offers healing, and brings peace to people. God forces good to come out of the evil. Jesus was constantly bringing good into the lives of those who were suffering by feeding the hungry, healing the sick, raising the dead, reaching out to the marginalized, and offering grace to all.

God is still bringing light into our darkness, offering comfort to us in our pain, walking alongside us in our journey of grief. Blessed are we who mourn, not because we mourn, but because God will comfort us. My prayer for you is that you will be able to sense God's presence, that God will enable you to get through this difficult time, and that God will empower you to keep putting one foot in front of the other on this marathon of grief.

If your experience is like mine, the comfort of God becomes most real in those God has brought alongside us to care for us. Often these are people who have suffered much. Yet all of them are willing to cry with us and to represent the God of compassion. Thanks be to God for those willing to walk with us in our pain.

The passage in Revelation quoted above assures us that God's comfort to us extends beyond this life. When God dwells with humans, God will eliminate death, dying, sadness, and tears. God will wipe away our tears as a mother gently dabs away the tears of her small child. God comforts us now by the Spirit, often through others and will continue to comfort those of us who mourn so that our sadness evaporates in eternity.

Moving Forward

1. Join a support group for those who are grieving or start your own.

2. Use the questions at the end of this book to continue the journey of grief.

3. Take a friend with you as you review the chapters in this book and renew your hope.

Prayer

Dear God, it was only through the dark night that we came to find your light. Had we not stumbled through the cold dark, we would not have come to the warmth of your hearth with frozen hands and heart. We are grateful for your comfort especially as we have experienced your love through those who have journeyed with us. May your grace and compassion fill us. May we sense your hand in ours. May your tears blend with ours. May we be willing to walk alongside others. Thank you for the promise that one day you will wipe away our tears and that death and mourning will be no more. Amen.

GROUP DISCUSSION QUESTIONS

A support group can be very helpful in dealing with grief. This book lends itself to both the individual working through grief and groups traveling the journey of grief together. A high level of trust and respect in such groups is essential. A group works best when everyone respects a variety of opinions related to what others choose to believe and to do with regard to grief.

Grief is very personal. There is no right or wrong way to grieve. While it will be very helpful for some people to talk about their pain, others will not be able to talk about their anguish in a group. Yet their presence may be important for them and others. Depending on the size of the group you may want to break into groups of two or three to discuss some of the more personal questions.

In addition to discussing the content of the chapters and sharing what suggestions you have tried, the questions below may help stimulate a meaningful discussion in a grief support group. These are hard questions because the work of grief is difficult. Being there for one another in a group process can help carry you through this terrible experience. The kind and loving presence of others can help us make it through this terrible time.

SESSION 1. HEARTBREAK (Chapters 1-5)
1. What has been the hardest part of grief for you? What has been most helpful in dealing with this heartache?

2. The author portrays his grief as being beaten by an angry gorilla. What images come to your mind for your experience of grief?

3. What has been hardest to let go of? What steps have you taken to help yourself let go?

4. How have you been able to express your emotions? Have there been times when you could not control your emotions? What were the reactions of others? How did you feel about yourself?

5. Have you begun new traditions or honored old ones to mark difficult days on the calendar? What has been helpful to you? What ideas do you have to mark the anniversary of the loss of your loved one?

6. What do you do on the hard days? Spend the day by yourself? With family? Friends? What would you recommend to others?

7. Do you sense God comforting you? If so, how? If not, talk about how that feels.

SESSION 2. HEARTBREAK (Chapters 6-10)
1. Share with others the impact of your loss in terms of your daily life and your future.

2. If you imagine grief as an object you could hold in your hands, what would it feel like?

3. How are you dealing with the ache of absence?

4. What feelings—positive or negative—have you had toward the one you lost?

5. How would you compare what you are going through now with other difficulties and challenges in your life?

6. How does this grief compare with other losses? What helped you get through previous times of sorrow?

7. Do you have regrets you are willing to share with the group? Are there things you wish you or others had done differently before your loved one passed away?

SESSION 3. ANGER AND GUILT (Chapters 11-15)

1. How has anger been part of your grief process? How have others reacted to your anger?

2. Who or what has been the focus of your anger?

3. Are you angry with God? How have you expressed anger toward God?

4. What helps you handle your anger?

5. What do you think you could have done that you did not do?

6. What brings you the most guilt? Was it something you did or said, something you failed to do?

7. How can you let go of the guilt? How can you forgive yourself?

8. In what ways did you let your loved one down? Do you think God forgives you? Do you think your loved one forgives you?

SESSION 4. FRIENDS AND MEMORIES (Chapters 16-20)

1. What things have people said that have been the most helpful?

2. What have people said that have angered or irritated you?

3. What things have people done for you that have been most beneficial to you as you experience this anguish?

4. How does it feel when someone listens to you share your story with them?

5. What are your favorite memories of your loved one?

6. What have you done to preserve your memories? Are there tangible ways you have sought to remember your loved one?

7. What is it like when you compare memories of your loved ones with those who knew him or her?

SESSION 5. WHY GOD? (Chapters 21-25)

1. If you believe that God could have saved your loved one from death and did not, how do you come to grips with that?

2. Do you believe God controls everything? Is there place in your theology for accidents or free will?

3. As you wrestle with why your loved one was taken, what ideas or answers have been most helpful?

4. In the story of Job, a righteous man suffers for no apparent reason. How do you see God's role in that story and in your own experience of loss?

5. How does your belief (or disbelief) in life after death relate to your understanding of your loved one's death?

SESSION 6. INJUSTICE, MURDER & SUICIDE (Chapters 26-30)

1. Was your loved one's death the result of the actions of someone else? If so, has justice happened for them?

2. If you have experienced injustice, talk about how that feels and what you would like to see happen.

3. What reasons can you give that some people live long and full lives while others die young?

4. If you have experienced suicide in your family, talk about that experience.

5. How has the experience of suicide changed you?

6. When you experience a suicide (or any death) how can you allow others to help you during this time?

7. In the light of your loss, what brings you peace?

SESSION 7. FAMILY, FUNERALS AND MEMORIALS (Chapters 31-38)

1. Did you have a service? What was it like? Was it helpful? What would you wish had been different? Any recommendations for the group?

2. What has it been like to see other family members suffer through this loss? How have you been able to grieve together?

3. How have family members been a help to you during this time of grief?

4. How did your family deal with conflicts after the loss?

5. How were your loved one's possessions handled after their passing? Do you have any advice to give from what you learned?

6. How do you feel about cremation?

SESSION 8. LIVING WITH THE NEW NORMAL (Chapters 39-43)
1. What has been the hardest part of the grieving process?

2. What has surprised you most about the grief you are experiencing?

3. What has been most helpful to you as you adjust to your new reality?

4. What has your experience been as you have encountered others who are grieving?

5. Have you made new traditions around your loved one's death that you would be willing to share?

SESSION 9. COMFORTING EACH OTHER (Chapters 44-47)
1. What has been the most helpful thing (practical or emotional) that someone else has done for you during this time of grief?

2. What advice would you give someone if they want to be helpful to a person who is grieving?

3. If you have been vulnerable with another about your loss, was that helpful to you or the other person?

4. How have others been present with you in a meaningful way?

5. How have people shared memories with you that have made you smile?

SESSION 10. GOD AND GRIEF (Chapters 48-52)
1. Have you ever thought of God as a grieving parent whose child died?

2. Do you believe that God cares about your loss?

3. How have you perceived God's presence or absence on your journey of grief?

4. Has your experience of grief caused you to question God's existence?

5. What clichés have you found to be inappropriate or hurtful?

SESSION 11. WHAT HAPPENS WHEN WE DIE? (Chapters 53-56)

1. Do you believe in an afterlife? If so, why? If not, why not?

2. In your opinion what happens when we die?

3. If you believe in heaven, how does that impact your grief?

4. How do you look at your own eventual death in light of your loss?

5. How is the idea of heaven a comfort to you?

SESSION 12. GRATITUDE AND HOPE (Chapters 57-65)

1. Are you able to be grateful in the midst of your grief? If so, how do you express gratitude?

2. Share ways your life was blessed by your loved one who has passed.

3. If you have a bulletin from the funeral or memorial service or an obituary, bring it to share with the group.

4. Compare experiences related to obituaries, preparations for services, services and receptions.

5. How have you dealt with happy occasions and holidays since your loss?

6. Does the resurrection of Christ Jesus offer you hope?

7. Does the concept of being a "blessed mourner" bring you any comfort? Does it offend you?

ABOUT THE AUTHOR

Rev. Samuel L. Wright, Sr., PhD, has served as a pastor, missionary and seminary professor. He currently serves as lead pastor of Plantation United Methodist Church in Plantation, Florida.

Made in the USA
Middletown, DE
31 March 2024

52363731R00195